donuts

donuts

recipes   Elinor Klivans

photographs   Lauren Burke

weldon**owen**

CONTENTS

making donuts AT HOME

From that first piece of leftover dough that was dropped into a pot of hot fat over a crackling fire, to the hole-in-the-middle glazed donuts of today, these popular sweets have been around for centuries. The name "doughnuts" probably evolved from the Dutch, who shaped dough scraps into knots or "dough knots" before frying. Fast forward to the present day, and the word is commonly shortened to the "donuts" seen on the neon signs of street-corner sweets shops.

Donuts are made in all shapes and sizes. Cream-filled puffs of yeast dough, two-bite donut holes, classic glazed or frosted rings, and light, irregularly shaped fritters are just some of the choices that this book has to offer. It begins with recipes for the classic yeast and cake donuts that we know so well. Among them are old-fashioned maple bars; fruit-filled jelly donuts; rings of dark, sweet, devil's food cake; and donut holes dusted with cinnamon sugar. These favorites are followed by a chapter featuring new and creative options that satisfy our modern appetite for variety. Chocolate rings flavored with spicy chile powder; crisp bacon-topped donuts; and puffs dipped in a salted caramel glaze and topped with chopped pecans are just some of the tempting choices. The last recipe chapter illuminates a whole world of donut traditions, offering regional and international specialties. From Mexico come honey-dipped *sopaipillas*; Italy contributes light ricotta *zeppole*; and Latin America lends its morning snack of long, crisp *churros* to dip in warm chocolate sauce; among other delights.

The most surprising fact about donuts is how easy they are to make at home. They are quick to mix, to form, and to cook, frying to crisp perfection in just a few minutes. Best of all, after cooling just briefly, it is time to eat the donuts. The recipes that follow will provide a wealth of choices to please any palate.

dough types

Although they come in many flavors and shapes, most donuts are made from one of three basic types of dough: yeast dough, cake dough, or *pâte à choux*. One common trait is that a plain donut, regardless of type of dough used, is not too sweet. It's the glazes, fillings, and toppings that supply most of the sweetness.

YEAST DOUGH Yeast-leavened donuts have a light, soft texture. After mixing, rolling, and cutting, they are set aside until they become soft and puffy. During this rising time the dough expands to form an airy texture that is emphasized when the donuts are fried.

CAKE DOUGH These donuts are leavened with baking powder, baking soda, or both, depending on the other dough ingredients, and both the mixing process and resulting texture is similar to that of a simple cake. Cake donuts are denser in texture than yeast-leavened donuts, but the extent of the crispiness depends on the ingredients. For example, a dough that contains cornmeal creates a crispier donut than one made with flour. Some donuts, such as drops and fritters, are made from a modified version of cake batter that is too moist and loose to roll and cut, but is added to the hot oil from a metal spoon to form large, irregular drops.

PÂTE À CHOUX This classic, French-style dough starts with a cooked mixture of milk or water, butter, salt, and flour. Eggs are beaten into the dough and then it is ready to be formed into the desired shapes, such as rings, ropes, or balls, and then deep-fried. The steam formed during frying creates the leavening and contributes to an especially light texture.

SPECIALTY DOUGHS Other donut batters don't fall into any of the above categories, but are the specialties of various countries around the world. For example, Mexican *sopaipillas* are made from a variation on piecrust. Indian-inspired donut balls use a large amount of dry milk powder to help absorb a spiced soaking syrup. New Orleans–style *calas* use a base of cooked rice to create a flavorful, textured breakfast fritter.

DOUGH LEAVENINGS

Quick-rise (also called rapid-rise, instant, or fast-rise) yeast has finer granules and acts more quickly than active dry yeast, make it the perfect choice for donuts. If using baking soda or baking powder, be sure that it is fresh. Buy a new supply if yours is more than 6 months old.

tools for making donuts

Making donuts at home does not necessarily mean purchasing new equipment; most of what you need you probably already have on hand in your kitchen. If you make donuts or other fried foods often, consider investing in a good-quality deep fryer, which eases the job of regulating the heat, controlling odors, and cleanup.

MIXING WITH A FOOD PROCESSOR

If you do not have a stand mixer, you can use a food processor with fine results: Following the sequence outlined in the recipe, add the dry ingredients to the work bowl and pulse 3 or 4 times to mix. Add the liquid ingredients and process for 20 to 30 seconds to form a dough. Transfer the dough to a bowl or a work surface, according to the recipe, and proceed as directed.

ELECTRIC MIXER A hand-held electric mixer or a stand mixer are necessary for making the donut dough. If you don't have a stand-mixer for making yeast dough, you can also use a food processor (see note at left).

ROLLING PIN AND CUTTERS A rolling pin is needed to roll the dough into a flat round before cutting. Donut cutters or round pastry cutters form the dough into its iconic round shapes.

DEEP FRYER An electric deep fryer maintains an even oil temperature and recovers its temperature quickly after donuts are added to the hot oil. Many deep fryers have a basket for quickly lifting the finished donuts out of the oil and a lid that prevents spattering and controls odors.

SAUTÉ PAN If you don't have a deep fryer, choose a sauté pan with straight sides that are at least 4½ inches (11.5 cm) high. The pan should also have a heavy bottom, which helps conduct heat evenly. When frying, take extra care that the hot oil does not spatter and burn you.

THERMOMETER A deep-frying thermometer ensures that the oil stays at the ideal frying temperature. It is equipped with a mercury bulb and a column attached to a metal casing and a clip that slips over the pan side to hold it securely. It is specially designed to register very high temperatures. Do not substitute an instant-read thermometer.

FRYING TOOLS A wide spatula or slotted spoon works well for sliding the donuts one at a time into the oil. The same spoon, a pair of tongs, or a wire skimmer are helpful tools for turning the donuts while frying and retrieving the finished donuts from the hot oil.

1

2

3

4

rolling and cutting donuts

Once you have mixed the ingredients to form a dough, gather the supplies you'll need for rolling and cutting, including a flat surface, plenty of flour, and a sturdy rolling pin. Be sure that your work surface is free of cracks or odors that could mar the donuts. A clean countertop or marble or plastic pastry board is ideal.

ABOUT DONUT CUTTERS

Similar to round cookie cutters, donut cutters feature a circular tube in the center so that both the large rings and the small holes can be cut in one step. If you don't have a donut cutter, two round pastry cutters—a large one to cut a circle and a small one to cut the hole—are a good option. A water glass and a sharp paring knife will also do the trick.

1 ROLL OUT THE DOUGH

Generously dust a work surface with all-purpose flour and place the dough in the center. Using a lightly floured rolling pin, roll out the dough into a circle 10 inches (25 cm) in diameter and ½ inch (12 mm) thick. Lift and turn the dough several times as you roll to prevent sticking. If the dough does stick, use a bench scraper or an icing spatula to loosen it, re-flour the work surface, and continue to roll. You can also refrigerate the dough for a few minutes to firm it, then continue to roll.

2 CUT OUT THE DONUTS

Using a 2½-inch (6-cm), 3-inch (7.5-cm), or another size donut cutter, cut out as many rounds as you can by firmly pressing the cutter into the dough; be sure the hole is cut out completely from the center. If the dough is sticking to the cutter, dip it lightly in flour. Gather the dough scraps, roll again, and cut out more rounds and holes. Discard the remaining scraps, as they will become tough from the rolling.

3 SET THE DONUTS ASIDE

If making yeast donuts, move them directly from the cutter to the prepared baking sheet, or use a wide spatula to transfer the donuts and holes. If making cake donuts, you can leave them on the work surface after cutting, but fry them as soon as possible to ensure the best texture.

4 LET THE DONUTS RISE (optional)

If making yeast donuts, cover the donuts and holes with a clean kitchen towel and let rise for 30 minutes. When ready, yeast donuts will look soft and puffy, but unlike many yeast doughs, they will not double in size.

deep-frying donuts

Deep-frying can seem daunting at first, but if you follow a few guidelines, it's easy to master. Use an oil that can be heated to a high temperature without burning, such as peanut or canola oil. And whether using a deep-fryer or sauté pan, testing the oil with a good deep-frying thermometer will ensure golden, crisp results.

WATCHING OIL TEMPERATURE

When donuts are fried at the proper temperature, they absorb little oil. If the frying temperature is too low, oil seeps into the dough, creating a soggy donut. If the oil is too hot, the outside of the donut will be overcooked. Most donuts cook best when the oil is maintained at 360°F (182°C) but there are some exceptions. Chocolate donuts cook at a lower 350°F (180°C) to prevent burning. Some light-textured donuts cook best at 340°F (170°C). Be sure to follow the recipe guidelines.

1 HEAT UP THE OIL

Pour the oil to a depth of 2 inches (5 cm) into a deep-fryer or deep, heavy sauté pan. Heat the oil in the deep-fryer according to the manufacturers' instructions. Some have a built-in temperature gauge, but it's still a good idea to check its accuracy with a deep-frying thermometer. If using a sauté pan, clip the thermometer onto the pan side and warm the oil over medium-high heat until it reaches the temperature called for in the recipe.

2 ADD THE DONUTS TO THE HOT OIL

When the oil reaches the desired temperature, use a wide spatula or slotted spoon to pick up a donut or hole from the baking sheet or work surface and slide it gently into the hot oil. Add 2–5 more donuts or holes, depending on the capacity of the fryer or pan, being careful not to splash the hot oil or crowd the frying vessel. The donuts should float to the top and puff to about double their size.

3 COOK THE FIRST BATCH

Deep-fry the donuts until dark golden on the first side (dark brown if making chocolate donuts), about 1½ minutes. Using tongs, a wire skimmer, or a slotted spoon, turn and fry until dark golden on the second side, about 1 minute longer. Transfer the fried donuts to paper towels to drain.

4 FRY THE REMAINING DONUTS

Repeat to fry the remaining donuts and holes, always allowing the oil to return to the initial frying temperature between batches. Be sure to watch the donuts carefully as they cook and never walk out of the kitchen. The time between just right and too much is just a matter of seconds.

1

2

3

4

the
CLASSICS

jelly-filled donuts

It seems we are never too old for the small burst of jelly hidden in the middle of these comfortingly familiar treats. Making your own donuts somehow only sweetens the surprise. Don't worry if the dough seems sticky—a soft dough makes a tender donut. Just keep your work surface generously floured.

Canola or peanut oil for brushing and deep-frying

Yeast Donut Dough (page 100)

⅔ cup (6 oz/185 g) best-quality strawberry jelly or seedless raspberry, apricot, or blueberry jam

½ cup (4 oz/125 g) superfine sugar

MAKES ABOUT 15 DONUTS

yeast DONUT

Line a baking sheet with waxed paper and brush the paper with oil. Line a second baking sheet with paper towels.

Turn the dough out onto a generously floured work surface. Using a floured rolling pin, roll out the dough into a circle about 10 inches (25 cm) in diameter and ½ inch (12 mm) thick. Using a 3-inch (7.5-cm) round pastry cutter, cut out as many rounds as possible. Use a wide spatula to transfer the donuts to the oiled paper. Gather up the scraps and repeat rolling and cutting out donuts. Cover the donuts with a clean kitchen towel and let rise for 30 minutes. The donuts should look soft and puffy, but will not double in size.

Pour oil to a depth of 2 inches (5 cm) into a deep-fryer or deep, heavy sauté pan and heat until the oil reads 360°F (182°C) on a deep-frying thermometer. Carefully lower 2–5 donuts into the hot oil and deep-fry until dark golden in color, about 1½ minutes. Turn over and cook until dark golden on the second side, about 1 minute longer. Transfer to the towel-lined baking sheet. Repeat to fry the remaining donuts, allowing the oil to return to 360°F between batches. (For more information on deep-frying, see page 14.)

Spread the sugar on a large plate or in a wide, shallow bowl. When the donuts are cool enough to handle, roll them in the sugar to coat on all sides. Fit a pastry bag with a ¼-inch (6-mm) round tip and spoon the jelly into the bag. Using the tip of a small, sharp knife, cut a ½-inch (12-mm) slit in the side of each donut. Press the tip of the pastry bag gently into the slits and pipe about 2 teaspoons of the jelly into each donut. Arrange the donuts on a platter and serve right away.

vanilla-glazed donuts

For many people, this iconic ringed cake, raised feather-light with yeast and covered with a sweet vanilla glaze, is the very definition of a donut. For a change of pace, Chocolate Glaze (page 107) can also be used; dip just the tops in the rich topping to avoid messy hands.

Canola or peanut oil for brushing and deep-frying

Yeast Donut Dough (page 100)

Vanilla Glaze (page 105)

MAKES ABOUT 15 DONUTS AND THEIR HOLES

Line a baking sheet with waxed paper and brush the paper with oil. Line a second baking sheet with paper towels.

On a generously floured work surface, roll out the dough into a circle 10 inches (25 cm) in diameter and ½ inch (12 mm) thick. Using a 3-inch (7.5-cm) round donut cutter, cut out as many donuts as possible. Transfer the donuts and holes to the oiled paper. Gather up the donut scraps and repeat rolling and cutting. (For more information on rolling and cutting, see page 13.) Cover the donuts and holes with a clean kitchen towel and let rise until soft and puffy, about 30 minutes.

Pour oil to a depth of 2 inches (5 cm) into a deep-fryer or deep, heavy sauté pan and warm over medium-high heat until it reads 360°F (182°C) on a deep-frying thermometer. Carefully lower 2–5 donuts or holes into the hot oil and deep-fry until dark golden, about 1½ minutes. Turn over and cook until dark golden on the second side, about 1 minute longer. Transfer to the towel-lined baking sheet. Repeat to fry the remaining donuts and holes, allowing the oil to return to 360°F between batches. (For more information on deep-frying, see page 14.)

When the donuts and holes are cool enough to handle but still warm, dip all sides in the vanilla glaze, letting any excess glaze drip back into the bowl. (You may not use all of the glaze, but this makes for easier dipping.) Place on a wire rack and let stand until the glaze sets, about 30 minutes. Arrange the donuts on a platter and serve right away.

yeast DONUT

old-fashioned buttermilk donuts

These classic cake donuts with a tang of buttermilk recall the golden piles in favorite bakeries of childhood memories. Leavened with baking soda and baking powder, they take minutes to mix. A combination of all-purpose flour and cake flour adds to the tender texture. Chilling the dough firms it for easy rolling.

1¼ cups (6½ oz/200 g) all-purpose flour

1 cup (4 oz/125 g) cake flour

1 teaspoon baking powder

½ teaspoon baking soda

½ teaspoon freshly grated nutmeg

½ teaspoon salt

1 large egg

cake DONUT

½ cup (4 oz/125 g) granulated sugar

½ cup (4 fl oz/125 ml) buttermilk

1 tablespoon unsalted butter, melted

1 teaspoon vanilla extract

Canola or peanut oil for deep-frying

Confectioners' sugar for dusting

MAKES ABOUT
10 DONUTS AND
THEIR HOLES

In a large bowl, sift together the flours, baking powder, baking soda, nutmeg, and salt. In another large bowl, using an electric mixer set on low speed (use the paddle attachment for a stand mixer), beat the egg and granulated sugar until creamy and pale in color. Add the buttermilk, melted butter, and vanilla and beat until well blended. Add the flour mixture and beat, still on low speed, just until the mixture comes together into a soft dough. Cover and refrigerate the dough until firm, at least 30 minutes and up to 1 hour.

Line a baking sheet with paper towels. Pour oil to a depth of 2 inches (5 cm) into a deep-fryer or deep, heavy sauté pan and warm over medium-high heat until it reads 360°F (182°C) on a deep-frying thermometer.

On a generously floured work surface, roll out the dough into a circle 10 inches (25 cm) in diameter and ½ inch (12 mm) thick. Using a 3-inch (7.5-cm) round donut cutter, cut out as many donuts as possible. Gather up the donut scraps and repeat rolling and cutting. (For more information on rolling and cutting, see page 13.)

Carefully lower 2–5 donuts or holes into the hot oil and deep-fry until dark golden, about 1½ minutes. Turn over and cook until dark golden on the second side, about 1 minute longer. Transfer to the towel-lined baking sheet to cool. Repeat to fry the remaining donuts and holes, allowing the oil to return to 360°F between batches. (For more information on deep-frying, see page 14.)

Arrange the donuts and holes on a platter. Using a fine-mesh sieve, dust generously with confectioners' sugar. Serve right away.

maple bars

Maple syrup adds an inviting golden color and a taste evoking Sunday breakfast to the thick glaze that gilds these rectangular donuts. Look for pure maple syrup, not artificially flavored pancake syrup. Use the longest sharp knife you have with a firm downward motion to cut the sticky dough into neat bar shapes.

Canola or peanut oil for brushing and deep-frying

Yeast Donut Dough (page 100)

Maple Glaze (page 106)

MAKES 12 BARS

Line a baking sheet with waxed paper and brush the paper with oil. Line a second baking sheet with paper towels.

Turn the dough out onto a generously floured work surface. Using a floured rolling pin, roll out the dough into a 12-by-8-inch (30-by-20-cm) rectangle. Using a sharp knife, cut the rectangle into 12 bars, each about 4 inches (10 cm) long and 2 inches (5 cm) wide. Use a wide spatula to transfer the bars to the oiled paper. Cover the bars with a clean kitchen towel and let rise for 30 minutes. The bars should look soft and puffy, but will not double in size.

Pour oil to a depth of 2 inches (5 cm) into a deep-fryer or deep, heavy sauté pan and warm over medium-high heat until it reads 360°F (182°C) on a deep-frying thermometer. Carefully lower 2–5 bars into the oil and deep-fry until dark golden in color, about 1½ minutes. Turn over and cook until dark golden in color on the second side, about 1 minute longer. Transfer to the towel-lined baking sheet. Repeat to fry the remaining bars, allowing the oil to return to 360°F between batches. (For more information on deep-frying, see page 14.)

When the bars are cool enough to handle, place them on a wire rack and drizzle each with the maple glaze, letting it drip down the sides. Let the bars stand until the glaze sets slightly, about 10 minutes. Serve right away.

yeast
DONUT

cider-glazed donuts

The flavors in these spiced donuts are echoed in the sweet apple-cider glaze, making them especially welcome during the apple harvest in autumn. Use the season's freshly pressed cider in the glaze and accompany the donuts with more cider—even hard cider—to drink.

1¼ cups (6½ oz/200 g) all-purpose flour

1½ teaspoons baking powder

¾ teaspoon ground cinnamon

½ teaspoon freshly grated nutmeg

½ teaspoon ground allspice

½ teaspoon salt

2 large eggs

½ cup (4 oz/125 g) granulated sugar

½ cup (4 fl oz/125 ml) whole milk

2 tablespoons unsalted butter, melted

1 teaspoon vanilla extract

Canola or peanut oil for deep-frying

MAKES ABOUT 10 DONUTS AND THEIR HOLES

cake DONUT

In a large bowl, sift together the flour, baking powder, cinnamon, nutmeg, allspice, and salt. In a large bowl, using an electric mixer set on low speed (use the paddle attachment for a stand mixer), beat the eggs and sugar until creamy and pale. Add half of the flour mixture and beat just until incorporated. Add the milk, melted butter, and vanilla and beat until well blended. Add the remaining flour mixture and beat, still on low speed, just until the mixture comes together into a soft dough. Cover and refrigerate the dough until firm to the touch, at least 30 minutes and up to 1 hour.

Line a large baking sheet with paper towels. Pour oil to a depth of 2 inches (5 cm) into a deep-fryer or deep, heavy sauté pan and warm over medium-high heat until it reads 360°F (182°C) on a deep-frying thermometer.

On a generously floured work surface, roll out the dough into a circle 10 inches (25 cm) in diameter and ½ inch (12 mm) thick. Using a 3-inch (7.5-cm) round donut cutter, cut out as many donuts as possible. Gather up the donut scraps and repeat rolling and cutting. (For more information on rolling and cutting, see page 13.)

Carefully lower 2–5 donuts or holes into the hot oil and deep-fry until dark golden, about 1½ minutes. Turn over and cook until dark golden on the second side, about 1 minute longer. Transfer to the towel-lined baking sheet. Repeat to fry the remaining donuts and holes, allowing the oil to return to 360°F between batches. (For more information on deep-frying, see page 14.)

CIDER GLAZE

2 cups (8 oz/250 g) confectioners' sugar

¼ **teaspoon ground cinnamon**

1 **teaspoon light corn syrup**

¼ **teaspoon vanilla extract**

3 **tablespoons apple cider, plus more as needed**

To make the cider glaze, in a bowl, stir together the confectioners' sugar, cinnamon, corn syrup, vanilla, and cider until well blended. Stir in 1–2 teaspoons more cider if needed to make a smooth glaze that is easy to spread, but thick enough to cling to the donuts.

Using a thin metal spatula, spread about 2 tablespoons of the glaze over the top of each donut. Spread the tops of the donut holes with 1–2 teaspoons of the glaze, or dip their tops in it. Place the donuts on a wire rack and let stand until the glaze sets, about 10 minutes.

Arrange the donuts and holes on a platter and serve right away.

cake
DONUT

SWEET TIP

Dress up just glazed donuts by sprinkling a tablespoon or two of colored sprinkles on top before the glaze sets.

sour cream—blueberry drops

These blueberry-studded, two-bite donut drops are made from a thick batter that, when fried, forms an ultra-crisp crust. A coating of cinnamon-sugar gives them a sweet-spicy finish. Be sure the batter completely covers the blueberries; any exposed berries could dislodge and float in the hot oil.

2 cups (10 oz/315 g) all-purpose flour

1¼ teaspoons ground cinnamon

½ teaspoon baking powder

½ teaspoon baking soda

½ teaspoon salt

¾ cup (6 oz/185 g) sour cream

1 large egg

⅔ cup (5 oz/150 g) granulated sugar

1 teaspoon vanilla extract

Canola or peanut oil for deep-frying

½ cup (2 oz/60 g) fresh or thawed frozen unsweetened blueberries

¼ cup (1 oz/30 g) confectioners' sugar

MAKES ABOUT 16 DROPS

cake DONUT

In a large bowl, sift together the flour, 1 teaspoon of the cinnamon, the baking powder, baking soda, and salt. In another large bowl, whisk together the sour cream, egg, granulated sugar, and vanilla until creamy and pale. Add the flour mixture and, using a large spoon, stir just until incorporated. The batter will be smooth.

Line a baking sheet with paper towels. Pour oil to a depth of 2 inches (5 cm) into a deep-fryer or deep, heavy sauté pan and warm over medium-high heat until it reads 340°F (170°C) on a deep-frying thermometer.

Using a metal spoon, scoop up a rounded tablespoonful of the batter and poke 3 blueberries into it, spacing them evenly. The blueberries should be completely covered by the batter. Drop gently into the hot oil, or scrape in using a second spoon. Repeat to add 4 or 5 more spoonfuls to the oil. Be sure not to overcrowd the pan. The drops should float to the top and puff to just about double their size. Deep-fry until dark golden on the first side, about 2 minutes. Using tongs, a wire skimmer, or a slotted spoon, turn and fry until dark golden on the second side, about 1½ minutes longer. Transfer to the paper towel-lined baking sheet to drain. Repeat to fry the remaining drops, allowing the oil to return to 340°F between batches. (For more information on deep-frying, see page 14.)

In a small bowl, combine the confectioners' sugar and the remaining ¼ teaspoon cinnamon and stir to mix well. Arrange the drops on a platter. Using a fine-mesh sieve, dust evenly with the cinnamon-sugar mixture. Serve right away.

toasted coconut donuts

These cake donuts represent a category called "sweet-milk donuts," which replaces the typical buttermilk with regular milk. The resulting mellow flavor complements the rich tropical sugars of the coconut glaze and crisp, toasted coconut coating, which in turn contrasts nicely with the soft crumb of the donuts.

2¼ cups (11½ oz/360 g) all-purpose flour

1½ teaspoons baking powder

½ teaspoon salt

2 large eggs

½ cup (4 oz/125 g) granulated sugar

½ cup (4 fl oz/125 ml) whole milk

2 tablespoons unsalted butter, melted

1 teaspoon vanilla extract

Canola or peanut oil for deep-frying

Coconut Glaze (page 105)

3 cups (12 oz/375 g) sweetened shredded coconut, toasted (page 100)

MAKES ABOUT
10 DONUTS AND
THEIR HOLES

cake DONUT

In a bowl, sift together the flour, baking powder, and salt. In a large bowl, using an electric mixer set on low speed (use the paddle attachment for a stand mixer), beat the eggs and sugar until creamy. Add half of the flour mixture and beat until incorporated. Add the milk, melted butter, and vanilla and beat until well blended. Add the remaining flour mixture and beat, still on low speed, just until the mixture comes together into a soft dough. Cover and refrigerate the dough until firm, at least 30 minutes and up to 1 hour.

Line a baking sheet with paper towels. Pour oil to a depth of 2 inches (5 cm) into a deep-fryer or deep, heavy sauté pan and warm over medium-high heat until it reads 360°F (182°C) on a deep-frying thermometer.

On a generously floured work surface, roll out the dough into a circle 10 inches (25 cm) in diameter and ½ inch (12 mm) thick. Using a 2½-inch (6-cm) or 3-inch (7.5-cm) round donut cutter, cut out as many donuts as possible. Gather up the donut scraps and repeat rolling and cutting. (For more information on rolling and cutting, see page 13.)

Carefully lower 2–5 donuts or holes into the hot oil and deep-fry until dark golden, about 1½ minutes. Turn over and cook until dark golden on the second side, about 1 minute longer. Transfer to the towel-lined baking sheet. Repeat to fry the remaining donuts and holes, allowing the oil to return to 360°F between batches. (For more information on deep-frying, see page 14.)

When the donuts and holes are cool enough to handle but still warm, dip all sides in the coconut glaze, letting any excess glaze drip back into the bowl. Place on a wire rack and let stand for about 10 minutes. Roll the donuts and holes in the toasted coconut to lightly coat all sides. Serve right away.

cinnamon-sugar donut holes

Here, donut holes are promoted from assistant to head honcho. To form the "holes," spoonfuls of dough are rolled between the palms of your hands into a crowd's worth of delicious round mini donuts. If not eaten right away, these are still tasty the next day; just warm them for 5-7 minutes in a 300°F (150°C) oven.

2¼ cups (11½ oz/360 g) all-purpose flour

2 teaspoons ground cinnamon

1½ teaspoons baking powder

½ teaspoon salt

2 large eggs

1½ cups (12 oz/375 g) granulated sugar

½ cup (4 fl oz/125 ml) whole milk

2 tablespoons unsalted butter, melted

1 teaspoon vanilla extract

Canola or peanut oil for brushing and deep-frying

MAKES ABOUT 40 HOLES

cake
DONUT

In a bowl, sift together the flour, 1 teaspoon of the cinnamon, the baking powder, and the salt.

In a large bowl, using an electric mixer set on low speed (use the paddle attachment for a stand mixer), beat the eggs and ½ cup (4 oz/125 g) of the sugar until creamy and pale. Add half of the flour mixture and beat just until incorporated. Add the milk, melted butter, and vanilla and beat until well blended. Add the remaining flour mixture and beat, still on low speed, just until the mixture comes together into a soft dough. Cover and refrigerate the dough until firm to the touch, at least 30 minutes and up to 1 hour.

Line a baking sheet with waxed paper and brush the paper with oil. Line a second baking sheet with paper towels. Pour oil to a depth of 2 inches (5 cm) into a deep-fryer or deep, heavy sauté pan and warm over medium-high heat until it reads 360°F (182°C) on a deep-frying thermometer.

Lightly oil the palms of your hands. Pull off about 1 tablespoon of the dough and roll it between your palms into a smooth ball about 1 inch (2.5 cm) in diameter. Place it on the oiled paper. Repeat to shape the remaining dough, spacing the dough balls 1-2 inches (2.5-5 cm) apart on the baking sheet. You should have about 40 dough balls.

Using tongs, transfer 6-8 donut holes, one or two at a time, from the baking sheet to the hot oil, sliding them in gently. Be sure not to overcrowd the pan. The donut holes should float to the top and puff to about double their size. Deep-fry until dark golden on the first side, about 1½ minutes. Using a slotted spoon, tongs, or a wire skimmer, turn and fry until dark golden on the second side, about 1 minute longer. Transfer the donuts to the towel-lined baking sheet to drain. Repeat to fry the remaining donut holes, allowing the oil to return to 360°F between batches. (For more information on deep-frying, see page 14.)

In a large bowl, combine the remaining 1 teaspoon cinnamon and 1 cup (8 oz/250 g) sugar and stir to mix well. Transfer to a large plate or a wide, shallow bowl. When the donut holes are cool enough to handle, but still slightly warm, roll them in the cinnamon-sugar to coat evenly on all sides. Arrange on a platter and serve right away.

cake
DONUT

cinnamon twists

Folding ropes of this pliable yeast dough and giving them a couple of twists is a simple task that yields a spectacular effect. The silky cinnamon glaze coats all of the swirled nooks and crannies of these perennial favorites. Serve them with freshly brewed coffee and you have the perfect morning treat.

¾ cup (6 fl oz/180 ml) whole milk

3 tablespoons unsalted butter

3¼ cups (16½ oz/515 g) all-purpose flour

⅓ cup (3 oz/90 g) granulated sugar

1½ teaspoons ground cinnamon

½ teaspoon salt

1 package (2½ teaspoons) quick-rise yeast

2 large eggs

½ teaspoon vanilla extract

Canola or peanut oil for brushing and deep-frying

Cinnamon Glaze (page 105)

MAKES 18 TWISTS

In a small saucepan over medium heat, combine the milk and butter and heat, stirring, until the butter melts and the mixture is hot but not boiling (about 125°F/52°C on an instant-read thermometer). Remove from the heat and set aside.

Fit a stand mixer with the paddle attachment. In the mixing bowl, combine 2½ cups (12½ oz/390 g) of the flour, the granulated sugar, cinnamon, salt, and yeast and beat on low speed to mix. Add the hot milk mixture, raise the speed to medium, and beat until well blended and smooth. Add the eggs and vanilla and beat until incorporated, about 2 minutes. Add the remaining ¾ cup (4 oz/125 g) flour and beat until well blended and smooth, about 1 minute longer. The dough will not pull away from the sides of the bowl and will still be somewhat sticky, but your finger should come out clean when you insert it into the center. (For a food processor method, see page 10.)

Scrape the dough into a large bowl and cover with a clean kitchen towel. Let stand in a warm place until well risen and increased in bulk (it may almost double in size), about 45 minutes.

Line a baking sheet with waxed paper and brush the paper with oil. Line a second baking sheet with paper towels.

Turn the dough out onto a generously floured work surface. Using a floured rolling pin, roll out the dough into an 18-by-9-inch (45-by-23-cm) rectangle. Using a large, sharp knife, cut the rectangle into 18 strips, each about

yeast DONUT

RECIPE CONTINUED ON PAGE 36

yeast DONUT

9 inches (23 cm) long and 1 inch (2.5 cm) wide. Bend each strip in half and twist the dough halves around each other 3 or 4 times to make a tight spiral. Pinch the ends to seal and place on the oiled paper. Cover with a clean kitchen towel and let rise for 30 minutes. The twists should look soft and puffy, but will not double in size.

Pour oil to a depth of 2 inches (5 cm) into a deep-fryer or deep, heavy sauté pan and warm over medium-high heat until it reads 360°F (182°C) on a deep-frying thermometer. Carefully lower 2–5 twists into the oil and deep-fry until dark golden, about 1½ minutes. Turn over and cook until dark golden on the second side, about 1 minute longer. Transfer to the towel-lined baking sheet. Repeat to fry the remaining donuts, allowing the oil to return to 360°F between batches. (For more information on deep-frying, see page 14.)

When the donuts are cool enough to handle but still warm, dip all sides in the cinnamon glaze, letting any excess glaze drip back into the bowl. (You may not use all of the glaze, but this makes for easier dipping.) Place on a wire rack and let stand until the glaze sets, about 30 minutes. Arrange on a platter and serve right away.

apple fritters

Apple fritters vary in form, from apple slices dipped in batter and fried to batters enriched with chopped apples, like these. The outside of these citrus-spiked fritters is roughly textured—just right for catching and absorbing the creamy cinnamon-apple glaze that is drizzled over the top.

1 cup (5 oz/150 g) all-purpose flour

¼ cup (2 oz/60 g) granulated sugar

1 teaspoon baking powder

¾ teaspoon ground cinnamon

½ teaspoon salt

⅓ cup (3 fl oz/80 ml) whole milk

1 large egg, lightly beaten

1 tablespoon fresh lemon juice

½ teaspoon grated lemon zest

½ teaspoon vanilla extract

1 large apple, cored, peeled, and finely chopped

Canola or peanut oil for deep-frying

Cinnamon-Apple Glaze (page 104)

MAKES ABOUT 24 FRITTERS

In a large bowl, whisk together the flour, sugar, baking powder, cinnamon, and salt. Make a well in the center of the flour mixture. Add the milk, egg, lemon juice and zest, and vanilla to the well and stir with a fork until well blended. Add the apple and stir just until evenly distributed.

Line a large baking sheet with paper towels. Pour oil to a depth of 2 inches (5 cm) into a deep-fryer or deep, heavy sauté pan and warm over medium-high heat until it reads 360°F (182°C) on a deep-frying thermometer.

Using a metal spoon, scoop up a rounded tablespoonful of the batter and drop into the hot oil, or scrape in using a second spoon. Repeat to add 5 or 6 more fritters to the oil. Be sure not to overcrowd the pan. The fritters should float to the top and puff to about double their size. Deep-fry until dark golden on the first side, about 2 minutes. Using tongs, a wire skimmer, or a slotted spoon, turn and fry until dark golden on the second side, about 1 minute longer. Transfer to the towel-lined baking sheet to drain. Repeat to fry the remaining fritters, allowing the oil to return to 360°F between batches. (For more information on deep-frying, see page 14.)

Arrange the fritters on a platter and, using a small spoon, drizzle about 1 teaspoon of the glaze over each. Let the glaze set for 10 minutes. Serve right away.

cake
DONUT

potato donuts

Old-fashioned and modern come together in these classic donuts: Mashed potatoes add an uncommonly smooth texture, and mace—a spice made from the outer covering of nutmeg berries with, logically, a mild nutmeg flavor—adds aroma and herbal hints. Salt and pepper add an unexpected savory kick.

2 cups (10 oz/315 g) all-purpose flour

1½ teaspoons baking powder

1 teaspoon salt

¾ teaspoon freshly ground pepper

½ teaspoon ground mace

cake DONUT

1 cup (7 oz/220 g) cooked, mashed, and cooled russet potato (about 1 medium potato)

⅔ cup (5 oz/150 g) granulated sugar

2 large eggs, lightly beaten

¼ cup (2 fl oz/60 ml) whole milk

2 tablespoons unsalted butter, melted

1 teaspoon grated lemon zest

Canola or peanut oil for deep-frying

MAKES 10–12 DONUTS AND THEIR HOLES

In a bowl, sift together the flour, baking powder, ¾ teaspoon of the salt, ¼ teaspoon of the pepper, and the mace. In another bowl, combine the potato, ⅓ cup (2½ oz/75 g) of the sugar, the eggs, milk, melted butter, and lemon zest. Using an electric mixer set on low speed (use the paddle attachment for a stand mixer), beat until blended. Add the flour mixture and beat until the mixture comes together into a sticky dough. Cover and refrigerate the dough until firm, at least 1 hour and up to 2 hours.

Line a baking sheet with paper towels. Pour oil to a depth of 2 inches (5 cm) into a deep fryer or deep, heavy sauté pan and warm over medium-high heat until it reads 360°F (182°C) on a deep-frying thermometer.

On a generously floured work surface, roll out the dough into a circle 10 inches (25 cm) in diameter and ½ inch (12 mm) thick. Using a 2½-inch (6-cm) or 3-inch (7.5-cm) round donut cutter, cut out as many donuts as possible. Gather up the donut scraps and repeat rolling and cutting. (For more information on rolling and cutting, see page 13.)

Carefully lower 2–5 donuts or holes into the hot oil and deep-fry until dark golden, about 1½ minutes. Turn over and cook until dark golden on the second side, about 1 minute longer. Transfer to the towel-lined baking sheet. Repeat to fry the remaining donuts and holes, allowing the oil to return to 360°F between batches. (For more information on deep-frying, see page 14.)

In a wide, shallow bowl, combine the remaining ⅓ cup (3 oz/90 g) sugar, ¼ teaspoon salt, and ½ teaspoon pepper and stir to mix well. When the donuts and holes are cool enough to handle, roll them in the sugar mixture to coat on all sides. Arrange on a platter and serve right away.

devil's food donuts

"Totally chocolate" perfectly describes these chocolate buttermilk donuts dipped in a luscious chocolate glaze. Pleasingly sticky, the glaze is the perfect consistency for taking them over the top: try adding some chocolate sprinkles, shaved bittersweet chocolate, or chocolate curls on the glaze before it sets.

1 cup (5 oz/150 g) all-purpose flour

1 cup (4 oz/125 g) cake flour

¼ cup (¾ oz/20 g) unsweetened cocoa powder, preferably Dutch process

1 teaspoon baking powder

½ teaspoon baking soda

½ teaspoon salt

1 large egg

½ cup (4 oz/125 g) granulated sugar

½ cup (4 fl oz/125 ml) buttermilk

1 tablespoon unsalted butter, melted

1 teaspoon vanilla extract

Canola or peanut oil for deep-frying

Chocolate Glaze (page 107)

MAKES ABOUT
12 DONUTS AND
THEIR HOLES

In a bowl, sift together the flours, cocoa powder, baking powder, baking soda, and salt. In a large bowl, using an electric mixer set on low speed (use the paddle attachment for a stand mixer), beat the egg and sugar until creamy and pale. Add the buttermilk, melted butter, and vanilla and beat until well blended and smooth. Add the flour mixture and beat, still on low speed, just until the mixture comes together into a soft dough. Cover and refrigerate the dough until firm, at least 30 minutes and up to 1 hour.

Line a large baking sheet with paper towels. Pour oil to a depth of 2 inches (5 cm) into a deep-fryer or deep, heavy sauté pan and warm over medium-high heat until it reads 360°F (182°C) on a deep-frying thermometer.

On a generously floured work surface, roll out the dough into a circle 10 inches (25 cm) in diameter and ½ inch (12 mm) thick. Using a 2½-inch (6-cm) round donut cutter, cut out as many donuts as possible. Gather up the donut scraps and repeat rolling and cutting. (For more information on rolling and cutting, see page 13.)

Carefully lower 2–5 donuts or holes into the hot oil and deep-fry until dark brown and crusty on the first side, about 1½ minutes. Turn over and cook until dark brown and crusty on the second side, about 1 minute longer. Transfer to the towel-lined baking sheet. Repeat to fry the remaining donuts and holes, allowing the oil to return to 360°F between batches. (For more information on deep-frying, see page 14.)

When the donuts and holes are cool enough to handle, dip the tops in the chocolate glaze, letting any excess glaze drip back into the bowl. Let stand until the glaze sets slightly, about 10 minutes. Serve right away.

cake
DONUT

new
FLAVORS

glazed orange blossoms

These unique, beautifully shaped, half-size donuts are created by cutting slits into the tops of balls of yeast dough; while rising, the sections open like the blossoms of a flower. Orange-flower water, distilled from orange blossoms, scents the dipping glaze, and orange zest in the dough marries the citrus flavors.

¾ cup (6 fl oz/180 ml) whole milk

3 tablespoons unsalted butter

3¼ cups (16½ oz/515 g) all-purpose flour

⅓ cup (3 oz/90 g) granulated sugar

½ teaspoon salt

1 package (2½ teaspoons) quick-rise yeast

2 large eggs

2 teaspoons grated orange zest

½ teaspoon vanilla extract

Canola or peanut oil for brushing and deep-frying

Orange-Flower Glaze (page 104)

MAKES ABOUT
18–20 DONUTS

In a small saucepan over medium heat, combine the milk and butter. Heat, stirring, until the butter melts and the mixture is hot but not boiling (about 125°F/52°C on an instant-read thermometer). Remove the pan from the heat and set aside.

Fit a stand mixer with the paddle attachment. In the mixing bowl, combine 2½ cups (12½ oz/390 g) of the flour, the sugar, salt, and yeast and beat on low speed to mix. Add the hot milk mixture, raise the speed to medium, and beat until well blended. Add the eggs, orange zest, and vanilla and beat until fully incorporated, about 2 minutes. Add the remaining ¾ cup (4 oz/125 g) flour and beat until well blended and smooth, about 1 minute longer. The dough will not pull away from the sides of the bowl and will still be somewhat sticky, but your finger should come out clean when you insert it into the center. (For a food processor method, see page 10.)

Scrape the dough into a large bowl and cover with a clean kitchen towel. Let stand in a warm place until well risen and increased in bulk (it may almost double in size), about 45 minutes.

Line a baking sheet with waxed paper and brush the paper with oil. Line a second baking sheet with paper towels.

Lightly grease the palms of your hands with oil. Pull off about 2 teaspoons of the dough and roll it between your palms into a smooth ball about 1½ inches (4 cm) in diameter. Place it on the greased paper. Repeat to

yeast
DONUT

RECIPE CONTINUED ON PAGE 46

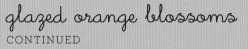

glazed orange blossoms
CONTINUED

yeast DONUT

shape the remaining dough, spacing the balls 1–2 inches (2.5–5 cm) apart on the baking sheet. You should have about 18–20 donut balls. Using a sharp knife, cut 2 evenly spaced horizontal slits and then 2 evenly spaced vertical slits into the top of each ball, making sure to penetrate halfway through the dough ball. Cover again with a clean kitchen towel and let rise for 30 minutes. The donuts should look soft and puffy, but will not double in size. The slits should spread open as the dough rises.

Pour oil to a depth of 2 inches (5 cm) into a deep-fryer or deep, heavy sauté pan and warm over medium-high heat until it reads 360°F (182°C) on a deep-frying thermometer. Carefully transfer 2–5 of the blossoms into the hot oil and deep-fry until dark golden, about 2 minutes. Using tongs, a wire skimmer, or a slotted spoon, turn over and cook for 1½ minutes longer. Transfer to the towel-lined baking sheet. Repeat to fry the remaining donuts, allowing the oil to return to 360°F between batches. (For more information on deep-frying, see page 14.)

When the donuts are cool enough to handle but still warm, dip the tops in the orange-flower glaze, letting any excess glaze drip back into the bowl. (You may not use all of the glaze, but this makes for easier dipping.) Place on a wire rack, glaze side up, and let stand until the glaze sets, about 30 minutes. Arrange on a platter and serve right away.

lemon—olive oil donuts

In addition to its appealing earthy flavor, using olive oil in the dough produces a donut with a unique texture: the inside is especially tender and the outside crisp and crusty. Lemon zest and black pepper introduce a sweet, tart, and peppery flavor, and the sugar, salt, and pepper coating carry out the theme.

2¼ cups (11½ oz/360 g) all-purpose flour

½ cup (4 oz/125 g) granulated sugar

1½ teaspoons baking powder

½ teaspoon salt

1 teaspoon freshly ground pepper

2 large eggs

⅓ cup (3 fl oz/80 ml) whole milk

¼ cup (2 fl oz/60 ml) extra-virgin olive oil

1½ teaspoons grated lemon zest

Canola or peanut oil for deep-frying

Sugar-and-Spice Topping (page 107)

MAKES ABOUT 10 DONUTS AND THEIR HOLES

In a large bowl, sift together the flour, sugar, baking powder, and salt. Stir in the pepper. Make a well in the center of the flour mixture. Add the eggs, milk, olive oil, and lemon zest to the well and stir with a fork until well blended. Cover the bowl with plastic wrap and refrigerate the dough until firm, at least 30 minutes and up to 1 hour.

Line a large baking sheet with paper towels. Pour oil to a depth of 2 inches (5 cm) into a deep-fryer or deep, heavy sauté pan and warm over medium-high heat until it reads 360°F (182°C) on a deep-frying thermometer.

On a generously floured surface, roll out the dough into a circle 10 inches (25 cm) in diameter and ½ inch (12 mm) thick. Using a 3-inch (7.5-cm) round donut cutter, cut out as many donuts as possible. Gather up the donut scraps and repeat rolling and cutting. (For more information on rolling and cutting, see page 13.)

Carefully lower 2–5 donuts or holes into the hot oil and deep-fry until dark golden, about 1½ minutes. Turn over and cook until dark golden on the second side, about 1 minute longer. Transfer to the towel-lined baking sheet. Repeat to fry the remaining donuts and holes, allowing the oil to return to 360°F between batches. (For more information on deep-frying, see page 14.)

When the donuts and holes are cool enough to handle, roll them in the topping to coat all sides. Arrange on a platter and serve right away.

cake
DONUT

pistachio-orange donuts

Chopped pistachios provide both a crunchy topping and a great complement to these orange-flavored donuts. Shelled roasted, salted pistachio nuts can be found in many kitchen specialty shops and in supermarkets. If you can only find unsalted nuts, sprinkle a few grains of salt lightly over the tops.

2¼ cups (11½ oz/360 g) all-purpose flour

1½ teaspoons baking powder

½ teaspoon salt

2 large eggs

½ cup (4 oz/125 g) granulated sugar

¼ cup (2 fl oz/60 ml) whole milk

¼ cup (2 fl oz/60 ml) fresh orange juice

2 teaspoons grated orange zest

2 tablespoons unsalted butter, melted

1 teaspoon vanilla extract

Canola or peanut oil for deep-frying

2½ cups (10 oz/315 g) roasted, salted pistachio nuts, finely chopped

MAKES ABOUT 10–12 DONUTS AND THEIR HOLES

In a bowl, sift together the flour, baking powder, and salt.

In a large bowl, using an electric mixer set on low speed (use the paddle attachment for a stand mixer), beat the eggs and sugar until creamy and pale. Add half of the flour mixture and beat just until incorporated. Add the milk, orange juice and zest, melted butter, and vanilla and beat until well blended. Add the remaining flour mixture and beat, still on low speed, just until the mixture comes together into a soft dough. Cover and refrigerate the dough until firm, at least 30 minutes and up to 1 hour.

Line a large baking sheet with paper towels. Pour oil to a depth of 2 inches (5 cm) into a deep-fryer or deep, heavy sauté pan and warm over medium-high heat until it reads 360°F (182°C) on a deep-frying thermometer.

On a generously floured work surface, roll out the dough into a circle 10 inches (25 cm) in diameter and ½ inch (12 mm) thick. Using an assortment of small, medium, and large round donut cutters, cut out as many donuts as possible. Gather up the donut scraps and repeat rolling and cutting. (For more information on rolling and cutting, see page 13.)

Carefully lower 2–5 donuts or holes into the hot oil and deep-fry until dark golden, about 1½ minutes. Turn over and cook until dark golden on the second side, about 1 minute longer. Transfer to the towel-lined baking sheet. Repeat to fry the remaining donuts and holes, allowing the oil to return to 360°F between batches. (For more information on deep-frying, see page 14.)

cake
DONUT

RECIPE CONTINUED ON PAGE 50

pistachio-orange donuts
CONTINUED

ORANGE GLAZE

6 tablespoons (3 oz/90 g) unsalted butter, melted

2½ cups (10 oz/315 g) confectioners' sugar

1 teaspoon vanilla extract

½ teaspoon almond extract

2 tablespoons fresh orange juice

3 tablespoons hot water, plus more as needed

1 teaspoon grated orange zest

To make the orange glaze, in a bowl, whisk together the melted butter, confectioners' sugar, vanilla and almond extracts, orange juice, and 3 tablespoons hot water until smooth. Whisk in 1–2 teaspoons more hot water if needed to give the glaze a thin consistency. Stir in the orange zest.

When the donuts and holes are cool enough to handle but still warm, dip the tops in the orange glaze, letting any excess glaze drip back into the bowl. (You may not use all of the glaze, but this makes for easier dipping.) Place on a wire rack and let stand until the glaze sets slightly, about 10 minutes. Put the pistachios on a large plate or in a wide, shallow bowl. Dip the tops of the donuts and donut holes in the nuts to coat the tops. Press gently with your fingertips to help them adhere, if necessary. Tap the donuts gently to shake off any loose nut pieces. Arrange on a platter and serve right away.

cake DONUT

meyer lemon custard donuts

Meyer lemons have a pure, clear, slightly sweet lemon taste. Their season runs from November through May, and they provide a great means for brightening up a winter dessert. If Meyer lemons are unavailable, use a mixture of half Eureka lemons and half oranges when making the glaze and custard.

Canola or peanut oil for brushing and deep-frying

Yeast Donut Dough (page 100)

Meyer Lemon Glaze (page 104)

Meyer Lemon Custard (page 102)

MAKES ABOUT
15 DONUTS

Line a baking sheet with waxed paper and brush the paper with oil. Line a second baking sheet with paper towels.

Turn the dough out onto a generously floured work surface. Using a floured rolling pin, roll out the dough into a circle about 10 inches (25 cm) in diameter and ½ inch (12 mm) thick. Using a 3-inch (7.5-cm) round pastry cutter, cut out as many rounds as possible. Use a wide spatula to transfer the donuts to the oiled paper. Gather up the scraps and repeat rolling and cutting. Cover the donuts with a clean kitchen towel and let rise for 30 minutes. The donuts should look soft and puffy, but will not double in size.

Pour oil to a depth of 2 inches (5 cm) into a deep-fryer or deep, heavy sauté pan and warm over medium-high heat until it reads 360°F (182°C) on a deep-frying thermometer. Carefully lower 2–5 donuts into the hot oil and fry until dark golden, about 1½ minutes. Turn over and cook until dark golden on the second side, about 1 minute longer. Transfer to the towel-lined baking sheet. Repeat to fry the remaining donuts, allowing the oil to return to 360°F between batches. (For more information on deep-frying, see page 14.)

When the donuts are cool enough to handle but still warm, dip the tops in the lemon glaze, letting any excess glaze drip back into the bowl. Place on a wire rack and let stand until the glaze sets, about 30 minutes.

Fit a pastry bag with a ¼-inch (6-mm) round tip and spoon the custard into the bag. Holding the unglazed bottom and using the tip of a small, sharp knife, cut a ½-inch (12-mm) slit in the side of each donut. Press the tip of the pastry bag gently into the slits and pipe about 1 tablespoon of the lemon custard into each donut. Serve right away.

yeast
DONUT

baked cherry streusel donuts

These round cake donuts have a crisp streusel topping and cakelike interior studded with tangy dried cherries. Unlike most donuts, they are baked in the oven instead of deep-fried, which highlights their fine-crumbed texture. The dough is very soft and must chill for at least an hour to be firm enough to roll.

2 cups (10 oz/315 g) all-purpose flour

1½ teaspoons baking powder

¼ teaspoon salt

1 large egg

½ cup (4 oz/125 g) granulated sugar

½ cup (4 fl oz/125 ml) whole milk

3 tablespoons unsalted butter, melted, plus butter for greasing

1 teaspoon vanilla extract

¼ teaspoon almond extract

¾ cup (3 oz/90 g) dried cherries, finely chopped

Streusel Topping (page 107)

½ cup (4 fl oz/125 ml) Thick Vanilla Glaze (page 105), warmed just until pourable

MAKES ABOUT
10 DONUTS

In a bowl, sift together the flour, baking powder, and salt. In a large bowl, using an electric mixer set on low speed (use the paddle attachment for a stand mixer), beat the egg and sugar until creamy and pale. Add the milk, melted butter, and vanilla and almond extracts and beat until well blended. Add the flour mixture and beat, still on low speed, just until the mixture comes together into a soft dough. Stir in the cherries. Cover and refrigerate the dough until firm, at least 1 hour and up to overnight.

Preheat the oven to 400°F (200°C). Line a baking sheet with parchment paper and butter the paper.

Turn the dough out onto a generously floured work surface. Using a floured rolling pin, roll out the dough into a circle about 10 inches (25 cm) in diameter and ½ inch (12 mm) thick. Using a 3-inch (7.5-cm) round pastry cutter, cut out as many rounds as possible. Gather up the scraps and repeat rolling and cutting.

Using a wide spatula, transfer the donuts to the buttered parchment paper, spacing them about 1½ inches (4 cm) apart. Using a pastry brush, brush the top of each donut with water. Sprinkle the streusel topping evenly over the tops and press gently with your fingertips to help the streusel adhere, if necessary. Bake until the tops are light golden, about 20 minutes. Transfer to a wire rack and let cool slightly.

When the donuts are cool enough to handle, press any bits of streusel that loosened during baking back in place. Using a spoon, drizzle the glaze in a back and forth motion lightly over the top of each donut. Serve right away.

cake DONUT

honey-cornmeal donuts

Imagine a honey-sweetened corn muffin with a super-crisp crust and you have an idea of what these hearty donuts deliver. Using cornmeal adds both a sweet, nutty flavor and a satisfying crunch. For more honey flavor, brush the outside of the cooked donuts with warm honey before dusting with confectioners' sugar.

cake DONUT

2 cups (10 oz/315 g) all-purpose flour

½ teaspoon baking powder

½ teaspoon baking soda

½ teaspoon salt

¾ cup (5 oz/150 g) stone-ground cornmeal

2 tablespoons unsalted butter, at room temperature

¼ cup (2 oz/60 g) granulated sugar

½ cup (6 oz/185 g) honey

1 large egg plus 1 large egg yolk

¼ cup (2 fl oz/60 ml) buttermilk

1 teaspoon grated lemon zest

Canola or peanut oil for deep-frying

Confectioners' sugar for dusting

MAKES ABOUT 12 DONUTS AND THEIR HOLES

In a bowl, sift together the flour, baking powder, baking soda, and salt. Stir in the cornmeal. In a large bowl, using an electric mixer set on low speed (use the paddle attachment for a stand mixer), beat the butter, granulated sugar, and honey until smooth. Add the egg and egg yolk and beat until well blended. Add half of the flour mixture and beat just until incorporated. Add the buttermilk and lemon zest and beat until well blended. Add the remaining flour mixture and beat, still on low speed, just until the mixture forms a soft dough.

Line a baking sheet with paper towels. Pour oil to a depth of 2 inches (5 cm) into a deep-fryer or deep, heavy sauté pan and warm over medium-high heat until it reads 340°F (170°C) on a deep-frying thermometer.

On a floured work surface, roll out the dough into a circle 10 inches (25 cm) in diameter and ½ inch (12 mm) thick. Using a 3-inch (7.5-cm) round donut cutter, cut out as many donuts as possible. Gather up the donut scraps and repeat rolling and cutting. (For more information on rolling and cutting, see page 13.)

Carefully lower 2–5 donuts or holes into the hot oil and deep-fry until dark golden, about 1½ minutes. Turn over and cook until dark golden on the second side, about 1 minute longer. Transfer to the towel-lined baking sheet. Repeat to fry the remaining donuts and holes, allowing the oil to return to 340°F between batches. (For more information on deep-frying, see page 14.)

Arrange the donuts and holes on a platter. Using a fine-mesh sieve, dust lightly with confectioners' sugar. Serve right away.

dulce de leche donuts

Dulce de leche, Spanish for "sweet milk," is a thick, sweet caramel filling or sauce from Central and South America. It is made by slowly cooking sweetened condensed milk until thick and a rich nut brown color—a perfect topping for yeast donuts. *Dulce de leche* is now widely available in well-stocked groceries.

¾ cup (6 fl oz/180 ml) whole milk

3 tablespoons unsalted butter

3¼ cups (16½ oz/515 g) all-purpose flour

½ cup (3½ oz/105 g) firmly packed light brown sugar

1 teaspoon ground cinnamon

½ teaspoon salt

1 package (2½ teaspoons) quick-rise yeast

2 large eggs

½ teaspoon vanilla extract

Canola or peanut oil for brushing and deep-frying

1¼ cups (10 oz/315 g) purchased *dulce de leche*

MAKES ABOUT
15 DONUTS AND
THEIR HOLES

In a small saucepan over medium heat, combine the milk and butter. Heat, stirring, until the butter is melted and the mixture is hot but not boiling (about 125°F/52°C on an instant-read thermometer). Remove the pan from the heat and set aside.

Fit a stand mixer with the paddle attachment. In the mixing bowl, combine 2½ cups (12½ oz/390 g) of the flour, the brown sugar, cinnamon, salt, and yeast and beat on low speed to mix. Add the hot milk mixture, raise the speed to medium, and beat until well blended. Add the eggs and vanilla and beat until fully incorporated, about 2 minutes. Add the remaining ¾ cup (4 oz/125 g) flour and beat until well blended and smooth, about 1 minute longer. The dough will not pull away from the sides of the bowl and will still be somewhat sticky, but your finger should come out clean when you insert it into the center. (For a food processor method, see page 10.)

Scrape the dough into a large bowl and cover with a clean kitchen towel. Let the dough stand until well risen and increased in bulk (it may almost double in size), about 45 minutes.

Line a baking sheet with waxed paper and brush the paper with oil. Line a second baking sheet with paper towels.

On a generously floured work surface, roll out the dough into a circle 10 inches (25 cm) in diameter and ½ inch (12 mm) thick. Using a 3-inch (7.5-cm) round donut cutter, cut out as many donuts as possible.

yeast DONUT

RECIPE CONTINUED ON PAGE 58

dulce de leche donuts
CONTINUED

Transfer the donuts and holes to the oiled paper. Gather up the donut scraps and repeat rolling and cutting. (For more information on rolling and cutting, see page 13.) Cover the donuts and holes with a clean kitchen towel and let rise until soft and puffy, about 30 minutes.

Pour oil to a depth of 2 inches (5 cm) into a deep-fryer or deep, heavy sauté pan and warm over medium-high heat until it reads 360°F (182°C) on a deep-frying thermometer. Carefully lower 2–5 donuts or holes into the hot oil and deep-fry until dark golden, about 1½ minutes. Turn over and cook until dark golden on the second side, about 1 minute longer. Transfer to the towel-lined baking sheet. Repeat to fry the remaining donuts and holes, allowing the oil to return to 360°F between batches. (For more information on deep-frying, see page 14.)

Using a thin metal spatula, spread a generous tablespoon of dulce de leche over the top of each donut. Spread the tops of the donut holes with about 1 teaspoon dulce de leche, or dip their tops in it. Arrange the donuts and holes on a platter and serve right away.

triple ginger donuts

The sweet-spicy flavor of ginger is layered in these donuts in three forms: both the grated fresh ginger and the ground spice are mixed into the dough. Chopped crystallized ginger is scattered over the vanilla glaze that tops the finished donuts. A microplane grater is a great tool for grating fresh ginger.

2¼ cups (11½ oz/360 g) all-purpose flour

2 teaspoons ground ginger

1½ teaspoons baking powder

1 teaspoon ground cinnamon

½ teaspoon salt

2 large eggs

⅔ cup (5 oz/150 g) granulated sugar

½ cup (4 fl oz/125 ml) whole milk

2 tablespoons unsalted butter, melted

1 teaspoon peeled and finely grated fresh ginger

1 teaspoon vanilla extract

Canola or peanut oil for deep-frying

Thick Vanilla Glaze (page 105)

⅔ cup (4 oz/125 g) crystallized ginger, finely chopped

MAKES ABOUT
10 DONUTS AND
THEIR HOLES

In a bowl, sift together the flour, ground ginger, baking powder, cinnamon, and salt. In a large bowl, using an electric mixer set on low speed (use the paddle attachment for a stand mixer), beat the eggs and sugar until creamy and pale. Add half of the flour mixture and beat just until incorporated. Add the milk, melted butter, fresh ginger, and vanilla and beat until well blended. Add the remaining flour mixture and beat, still on low speed, just until the mixture comes together into a soft dough. Cover and refrigerate the dough until firm, at least 30 minutes and up to 1 hour.

Line a baking sheet with paper towels. Pour oil to a depth of 2 inches (5 cm) into a deep-fryer or deep, heavy sauté pan and heat until it reads 360°F (182°C) on a deep-frying thermometer.

On a floured work surface, roll out the dough into a circle 10 inches (25 cm) in diameter and ½ inch (12 mm) thick. Using a 3-inch (7.5-cm) round donut cutter, cut out as many donuts as possible. Gather up the donut scraps and repeat rolling and cutting. (For more information on rolling and cutting, see page 13.)

Carefully lower 2–5 donuts or holes into the oil and deep-fry until dark golden, about 1½ minutes. Turn over and cook until dark golden on the second side, about 1 minute longer. Transfer to the towel-lined baking sheet. Repeat to fry the remaining donuts and holes, allowing the oil to return to 360°F between batches. (For more information on deep-frying, see page 14.)

Spread the glaze over the top of each donut and hole. Place on a wire rack and let stand until the glaze sets slightly, about 10 minutes. Sprinkle the crystallized ginger over the tops of the donuts and holes and serve right away.

salted caramel—pecan donuts

These donuts are an example of the delicious practice of mixing salty and sweet ingredients. The recipe uses an easy method of making caramel, which is to simply boil brown sugar, cream, and corn syrup together—the corn syrup keeps the mixture smooth because no sugar crystals will form.

¾ cup (6 fl oz/180 ml) whole milk

3 tablespoons unsalted butter

3¼ cups (16½ oz/515 g) all-purpose flour

½ cup (3½ oz/105 g) firmly packed light brown sugar

1 teaspoon ground cinnamon

½ teaspoon salt

1 package (2½ teaspoons) quick-rise yeast

2 large eggs

½ teaspoon vanilla extract

Canola or peanut oil for brushing and deep-frying

Caramel Glaze (page 106)

1¼ cups (5 oz/150 g) pecans, toasted (page 100)

½ teaspoon kosher or sea salt

MAKES ABOUT 15 DONUTS AND THEIR HOLES

In a small saucepan over medium heat, combine the milk and butter and heat, stirring, until the butter melts and the mixture is hot but not boiling (about 125°F/52°C on an instant-read thermometer). Remove from the heat.

Fit a stand mixer with the paddle attachment. In the mixing bowl, combine 2½ cups (12½ oz/390 g) of the flour, the brown sugar, cinnamon, salt, and yeast and beat on low speed to mix. Add the hot milk mixture, raise the speed to medium, and beat until well blended and smooth. Add the eggs and vanilla and beat until fully incorporated, about 2 minutes. Add the remaining ¾ cup (4 oz/125 g) flour and beat until well blended and smooth, about 1 minute longer. The dough will not pull away from the sides of the bowl and will still be somewhat sticky, but your finger should come out clean when you insert it into the center. (For a food processor method, see page 10.)

Scrape the dough into a large bowl and cover the dough with a clean kitchen towel. Let stand until well risen and increased in bulk (it may almost double in size), about 45 minutes.

Line a baking sheet with waxed paper and brush the paper with oil. Line a second baking sheet with paper towels.

On a generously floured work surface, roll out the dough into a circle 10 inches (25 cm) in diameter and ½ inch (12 mm) thick. Using a 3-inch (7.5-cm) round donut cutter, cut out as many donuts as possible. Transfer the donuts and holes to the oiled paper. Gather up the donut scraps and

yeast DONUT

RECIPE CONTINUED ON PAGE 62

salted caramel–pecan donuts
CONTINUED

repeat rolling and cutting. (For more information on rolling and cutting, see page 13.) Cover the donuts and holes with a clean kitchen towel and let rise until soft and puffy, about 30 minutes.

Pour oil to a depth of 2 inches (5 cm) into a deep-fryer or deep, heavy sauté pan and warm over medium-high heat until it reads 360°F (182°C) on a deep-frying thermometer. Carefully lower 2–5 donuts or holes into the hot oil and deep-fry until dark golden, about 1½ minutes. Turn over and cook until dark golden on the second side, about 1 minute longer. Transfer to the towel-lined baking sheet. Repeat to fry the remaining donuts and holes, allowing the oil to return to 360°F between batches. (For more information on deep-frying, see page 14.)

Using a thin metal spatula, spread a thin layer of the caramel glaze over the top of each donut. (If the caramel is too thick, heat over low heat until spreadable, 2–3 minutes.) Spread the tops of the donut holes with a thin layer of glaze, or dip their tops in it. Dip the glazed portions of the donuts and holes in the toasted pecans. Press gently with your fingertips to help them adhere, if necessary. Tap the donuts gently to shake off any loose pecan pieces. Sprinkle with the salt. Serve right away.

yeast
DONUT

sticky toffee donuts

These donuts are reminiscent of the famed English dessert, sticky toffee pudding. The shiny toffee glaze that covers these donuts makes them a standout in any assortment, as do the sweet and chewy bits of dried dates in the dough. The decadent sauce will thicken as it cooks and thicken even more as it cools.

2¼ cups (11½ oz/360 g) all-purpose flour

1½ teaspoons baking powder

½ teaspoon salt

2 large eggs

⅓ cup (2½ oz/75 g) firmly packed dark brown sugar

½ cup (4 fl oz/125 ml) whole milk

2 tablespoons unsalted butter, melted

1 teaspoon vanilla extract

⅔ cup (4 oz/125 g) pitted dates, finely chopped

Canola or peanut oil for deep-frying

Sticky Toffee Glaze (page 106)

MAKES ABOUT 12 DONUTS AND THEIR HOLES

In a bowl, sift together the flour, baking powder, and salt. In a large bowl, using an electric mixer set on low speed (use the paddle attachment for a stand mixer), beat the eggs and brown sugar until creamy. Add half of the flour mixture and beat just until incorporated. Add the milk, melted butter, and vanilla and beat until well blended. Add the remaining flour mixture and beat, still on low speed, just until the mixture comes together into a soft dough. Stir in the dates. Cover and refrigerate the dough until firm, at least 30 minutes and up to 1 hour.

Line a large baking sheet with paper towels. Pour oil to a depth of 2 inches (5 cm) into a deep-fryer or deep, heavy sauté pan and warm over medium-high heat until it reads 360°F (182°C) on a deep-frying thermometer.

On a floured work surface, roll out the dough into a circle 10 inches (25 cm) in diameter and ½ inch (12 mm) thick. Using a 3-inch (7.5-cm) round donut cutter, cut out as many donuts as possible. Gather up the donut scraps and repeat rolling and cutting. (For more information on rolling and cutting, see page 13.)

Carefully lower 2–5 donuts or holes into the hot oil and deep-fry until dark golden, about 1½ minutes. Turn over and cook until dark golden on the second side, about 1 minute longer. Transfer to the towel-lined baking sheet. Repeat to fry the remaining donuts and holes, allowing the oil to return to 360°F between batches. (For more information on deep-frying, see page 14.)

When the donuts and holes are cool enough to handle, dip the top half into the glaze, letting any excess drip back into the bowl. Place on a wire rack and let stand until slightly set, about 15 minutes. The glaze will remain sticky. Serve right away.

cake DONUT

maple-bacon donuts

These crowd-pleasing donuts feature a maple glaze that is adorned with crisp pieces of bacon. The bacon is dipped into maple syrup before it's baked, raising the bar on the favorite sweet-and-salty combination to new heights. The sweet bacon also makes a good salad crumble or a tasty variation on the BLT sandwich.

¼ cup (3½ oz/85 g) maple syrup

5 strips thinly sliced bacon (about 4 oz/125 g)

2¼ cups (11½ oz/360 g) all-purpose flour

1½ teaspoons baking powder

½ teaspoon salt

2 large eggs

¼ cup (2 oz/60 g) granulated sugar

¼ cup (2 oz/60 g) firmly packed brown sugar

½ cup (4 fl oz/125 ml) whole milk

2 tablespoons unsalted butter, melted

1 teaspoon vanilla extract

Canola or peanut oil for deep-frying

Maple Glaze (page 106)

MAKES ABOUT
10 DONUTS AND
THEIR HOLES

Preheat the oven to 375°F (190°C). Line a large rimmed baking sheet with aluminum foil. Line a plate with paper towels.

Pour the maple syrup into a shallow bowl and dip the bacon slices in the syrup to coat on all sides. Arrange the slices on the baking sheet, laying them flat and placing them at least 1 inch (2.5 cm) apart. Bake until the bacon is browned and crisp, about 20 minutes. Remove from the oven and transfer to the towel-lined plate to drain. Blot the tops with additional paper towels. The bacon will get crisper as it cools. When cool, break or cut the bacon into ¼–½-inch (4–6-mm) pieces. Set aside.

In a bowl, sift together the flour, baking powder, and salt. In a large bowl, using an electric mixer set on low speed (use the paddle attachment for a stand mixer), beat the eggs, granulated sugar, and brown sugar until creamy. Add half of the flour mixture and beat just until incorporated. Add the milk, melted butter, and vanilla and beat until well blended. Add the remaining flour mixture and beat, still on low speed, just until the mixture comes together into a soft dough. Cover and refrigerate the dough until firm, at least 30 minutes and up to 1 hour.

Line a baking sheet with paper towels. Pour oil to a depth of 2 inches (5 cm) into a deep-fryer or deep, heavy sauté pan and warm over medium-high heat until it reads 360°F (182°C) on a deep-frying thermometer.

cake
DONUT

RECIPE CONTINUED ON PAGE 66

maple-bacon donuts
CONTINUED

On a floured work surface, roll out the dough into a circle 10 inches (25 cm) in diameter and ½ inch (12 mm) thick. Using a 3-inch (7.5-cm) round donut cutter, cut out as many donuts as possible. Gather up the donut scraps and repeat rolling and cutting. (For more information on rolling and cutting, see page 13.)

Carefully lower 2–5 donuts or holes into the oil and deep-fry until dark golden, about 1½ minutes. Turn over and cook until dark golden on the second side, about 1 minute longer. Transfer to the towel-lined baking sheet. Repeat to fry the remaining donuts and holes, allowing the oil to return to 360°F between batches. (For more information on deep-frying, see page 14.)

Using a thin metal spatula, spread about 2 tablespoons of the maple glaze over the top of each donut. Spread the tops of the donut holes with 1–2 teaspoons of the glaze, or dip their tops in it. Sprinkle the bacon pieces over the glazed portions of the donuts and donut holes and press gently with your fingertips to help them adhere, if necessary. Arrange the donuts and their holes on a platter and serve right away.

cake
DONUT

chocolate-hazelnut fritters

Chocolate and hazelnuts seem to bring out the best in each other. These fritters start with a cocoa powder and hazelnut dough, and then the finished donuts are drizzled with melted chocolate and sprinkled with chopped hazelnuts. To save time, look for skinless hazelnuts in well-stocked markets.

¾ cup (4 oz/125 g) plus 2 tablespoons all-purpose flour

¼ cup (¾ oz/20 g) unsweetened cocoa powder, preferably Dutch process

¼ cup (2 oz/60 g) granulated sugar

½ teaspoon baking powder

½ teaspoon salt

½ cup (4 fl oz/125 ml) sparkling water

1 large egg, lightly beaten

½ teaspoon vanilla extract

⅔ cup (3 oz/90 g) hazelnuts, toasted (page 100) and chopped

Canola or peanut oil for deep-frying

4 oz (125 g) semisweet chocolate, chopped

MAKES ABOUT 16 FRITTERS

In a large bowl, whisk together the flour, cocoa powder, sugar, baking powder, and salt. Make a well in the center of the flour mixture. Add the sparkling water, egg, and vanilla to the well and stir with a fork until well blended. Add ¼ cup (1 oz/30 g) of the hazelnuts and stir just until evenly distributed. Set aside.

Line a baking sheet with paper towels. Pour oil to a depth of 2 inches (5 cm) into a deep-fryer or deep, heavy sauté pan and warm over medium-high heat until it reads 360°F (182°C) on a deep-frying thermometer.

Using a metal spoon, scoop up a rounded tablespoonful of the batter and drop into the hot oil, or scrape in using a second spoon. Repeat to add 5 or 6 more spoonfuls to the oil. Be sure not to overcrowd the pan. The fritters should float to the top and puff to about double in size. Deep-fry until dark brown and crusty on the first side, about 2 minutes. Using tongs, a wire skimmer, or a slotted spoon, turn and fry until dark brown and crusty on the second side, about 1 minute longer. Transfer to the towel-lined baking sheet to drain. Repeat to fry the remaining fritters, allowing the oil to return to 360°F between batches.

Put the chocolate in the top part of a double boiler and set over (but not touching) barely simmering water. Heat, stirring often, until the chocolate melts. Remove from the heat and let cool slightly. Using a small spoon, drizzle about 1 teaspoon of the melted chocolate over each fritter. Let stand until the chocolate sets slightly, about 5 minutes. Put the remaining hazelnuts in a small bowl and dip the chocolate-coated portions of the fritters in the nuts, pressing gently to help them adhere. Serve right away.

cake
DONUT

brown sugar donuts

The dough for these donuts has an appealing light brown color that deepens into a striking dark golden ring that hints at the orange and spice flavors within. The combination of flavors in the treats—cinnamon, citrus, and caramel-like brown sugar—evokes a hot drink enjoyed by a cozy fire on a cold winter evening.

¾ cup (6 fl oz/180 ml) whole milk

3 tablespoons unsalted butter

3¼ cups (16½ oz/515 g) all-purpose flour

⅓ cup (2½ oz/75 g) firmly packed light brown sugar

1 teaspoon ground cinnamon

½ teaspoon salt

1 package (2½ teaspoons) quick-rise yeast

2 large eggs

2 teaspoons grated orange zest

Canola or peanut oil for brushing and deep-frying

Cinnamon-Orange Glaze (page 104)

MAKES 15–18 DONUTS AND THEIR HOLES

In a small saucepan over medium heat, combine the milk and butter and heat, stirring, until the butter is melted and the mixture is hot but not boiling (125°F/52°C on an instant-read thermometer). Remove from the heat.

Fit a stand mixer with a paddle attachment. In the mixing bowl, combine 2½ cups (12½ oz/390 g) of the flour, the brown sugar, cinnamon, salt, and yeast and beat on low speed to mix. Add the hot milk mixture, raise the speed to medium, and beat until well blended. Add the eggs and orange zest and beat until fully incorporated, about 2 minutes. Add the remaining ¾ cup (4 oz/125 g) flour and beat until well blended and smooth, about 1 minute longer. The dough will not pull away from the sides of the bowl and will still be somewhat sticky, but your finger should come out clean when you insert it into the center. (For a food processor method, see page 10.)

Scrape the dough into a large bowl and cover the dough with a clean kitchen towel. Let stand until the dough is well risen and increased in bulk (it may almost double in size), about 45 minutes.

Line a baking sheet with waxed paper and brush the paper with oil. Line a second baking sheet with paper towels.

On a generously floured work surface, roll out the dough into a circle 10 inches (25 cm) in diameter and ½ inch (12 mm) thick. Using a 2½-inch (6-cm) or 3-inch (7.5-cm) round donut cutter, cut out as many donuts as possible. Transfer the donuts and holes to the oiled paper. Gather up the

RECIPE CONTINUED ON PAGE 70

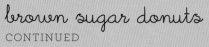

brown sugar donuts
CONTINUED

donut scraps and repeat rolling and cutting. (For more information on rolling and cutting, see page 13). Cover the donuts and holes with a clean kitchen towel and let rise until soft and puffy, about 30 minutes.

Pour oil to a depth of 2 inches (5 cm) into a deep-fryer or deep, heavy sauté pan and warm over medium-high heat until it reads 360°F (182°C) on a deep-frying thermometer. Carefully lower 3 or 4 donuts or holes into the hot oil and deep-fry until dark golden, about 1½ minutes. Turn over and cook until dark golden on the second side, about 1 minute longer. Transfer to the towel-lined baking sheet. Repeat to fry the remaining donuts and holes, allowing the oil to return to 360°F between batches. (For more information on deep-frying, see page 14.)

Using a thin metal spatula, spread about 2 tablespoons of the glaze over the top of each donut. Spread the tops of the donut holes with 1–2 teaspoons of the glaze, or dip their tops in it. Let stand until the glaze is slightly set, about 10 minutes. Arrange the donuts and holes on a platter and serve right away.

yeast
DONUT

banana cream donuts

To understand what these custard-filled treats have to offer, think: banana cream pie in a donut. Ripe, soft bananas are mashed into a thick vanilla custard to make a smooth, chilled filling. A dip in a light vanilla glaze doubles the decadence and lends a beautiful finish to the hard-to-resist treats.

Canola or peanut oil for brushing and deep-frying

Yeast Donut Dough (page 100)

Vanilla Glaze (page 105)

Banana Custard (page 102)

MAKES ABOUT
15 DONUTS

Line a baking sheet with waxed paper and brush the paper with oil. Line a second baking sheet with paper towels.

Turn the dough out onto a generously floured work surface. Using a floured rolling pin, roll out the dough into a circle about 10 inches (25 cm) in diameter and ½ inch (12 mm) thick. Using a 3-inch (7.5-cm) round pastry cutter, cut out as many rounds as possible. Use a wide spatula to transfer the donuts to the oiled paper. Gather up the scraps and repeat rolling and cutting. Cover the donuts with a clean kitchen towel and let rise for 30 minutes. The donuts should look soft and puffy, but will not double in size.

Pour oil to a depth of 2 inches (5 cm) into a deep-fryer or deep, heavy sauté pan and warm over medium-high heat until it reads 360°F (182°C) on a deep-frying thermometer. Carefully lower 2–5 donuts into the hot oil and fry until dark golden in color, about 1½ minutes. Turn over and cook until dark golden in color on the second side, about 1 minute longer. Transfer to the towel-lined baking sheet. Repeat to fry the remaining donuts, allowing the oil to return to 360°F between batches. (For more information on deep-frying, see page 14.)

When the donuts are cool enough to handle but still warm, dip all sides in the vanilla glaze, letting any excess glaze drip back into the bowl. Place on a wire rack and let stand until the glaze sets, about 30 minutes.

Fit a pastry bag with a ¼-inch (6-mm) round tip and spoon the custard into the bag. Holding the bottom and using the tip of a small, sharp knife, cut a ½-inch (12-mm) slit in the side of each donut. Press the tip into the slit and pipe 1 tablespoon of the custard into each donut. Serve right away.

chocolate—almond crunch donuts

Soft and crunchy, chocolatey and nutty: these donuts have it all. Cocoa powder adds deep chocolate flavor and color to these uniquely shaped treats, while sugar-glazed toasted almonds contribute a crisp topping. Almond Crunch is also delicious sprinkled over bowls of ice cream.

¾ cup (6 fl oz/180 ml) whole milk

3 tablespoons unsalted butter

3 cups (15 oz/470 g) all-purpose flour

¼ cup (¾ oz/20 g) unsweetened cocoa powder, preferably Dutch process

⅓ cup (3 oz/90 g) granulated sugar

½ teaspoon salt

1 package (2½ teaspoons) quick-rise yeast

2 large eggs

½ teaspoon vanilla extract

Canola or peanut oil for brushing and deep-frying

Chocolate Glaze (page 107)

Almond Crunch (page 107)

MAKES ABOUT 16 DONUTS AND THEIR HOLES

In a small saucepan over medium heat, combine the milk and butter. Heat, stirring, until the butter is melted and the mixture is hot but not boiling (about 125°F/52°C on an instant-read thermometer). Remove from the heat. Set aside.

Fit a stand mixer with the paddle attachment. In the mixing bowl, combine 2½ cups (12½ oz/390 g) of the flour, the cocoa powder, sugar, salt, and yeast and beat on low speed to mix. Add the hot milk mixture, raise the speed to medium, and beat until well blended. Add the eggs and vanilla and beat until incorporated, about 2 minutes. Add the remaining ½ cup (2½ oz/7.5 g) flour and beat until well blended and smooth, about 1 minute longer. The dough will not pull away from the sides of the bowl and will still be somewhat sticky, but your finger should come out clean when you insert it into the center. (For a food processor method, see page 10.)

Scrape the dough into a large bowl and cover with a clean kitchen towel. Let stand until the dough is well risen and increased in bulk (it may almost double in size), about 45 minutes.

Line a baking sheet with waxed paper and brush the paper with oil. Line a second baking sheet with paper towels.

On a floured work surface, roll out the dough into a 12-by-12-inch (30-by-30-cm) square. Using a long knife, cut the dough into sixteen 3-inch (7.5-cm) squares. Using a paring knife, cut out 1-inch (2.5-cm) square holes. Transfer

yeast DONUT

RECIPE CONTINUED ON PAGE 74

chocolate-almond crunch donuts
CONTINUED

the donuts and holes to the oiled paper. Gather up the donut scraps and repeat rolling and cutting. (To make round donuts, follow the instructions for rolling and cutting on page 13.) Cover the donuts and holes with a clean kitchen towel and let rise until soft and puffy, about 30 minutes.

Pour oil to a depth of 2 inches (5 cm) into a deep-fryer or deep, heavy sauté pan and warm over medium-high heat until it reads 350°F (180°C) on a deep-frying thermometer. Carefully lower 2–5 donuts or holes into the hot oil and deep-fry until dark brown and crusty on the first side, about 1½ minutes. Turn over and cook until dark brown and crusty on the second side, about 1 minute longer. Transfer to the towel-lined baking sheet. Repeat to fry the remaining donuts and holes, allowing the oil to return to 350°F between batches. (For more information on deep-frying, see page 14.)

When the donuts and holes are cool enough to handle, dip the tops in the chocolate glaze, letting any excess glaze drip back into the bowl. (You may not use all of the glaze, but this makes for easier dipping.) Place on a wire rack and let stand until the glaze sets slightly, about 10 minutes. Sprinkle a generous tablespoon of the almond crunch over the top of each donut, pressing gently with your fingertips to help it adhere, if necessary. Arrange on a platter and serve right away.

yeast
DONUT

chocolate-chile donuts

Ancho chile powder has a deep flavor and a subtle heat that marries well with chocolate, and likewise these chocolate donuts. If desired, you can increase the amount of chile powder to suit your taste, but take care that the chiles do not overpower the chocolate and create nothing but a hot, spicy result.

1 cup (5 oz/150 g) all-purpose flour

1 cup (4 oz/125 g) cake flour

¼ cup (¾ oz/20 g) unsweetened cocoa powder, preferably Dutch process

1 teaspoon baking powder

½ teaspoon baking soda

½ teaspoon salt

1 large egg

½ cup (4 oz/125 g) granulated sugar

½ cup (4 fl oz/125 ml) buttermilk

1 tablespoon unsalted butter, melted

2¼ teaspoons ancho chile powder

1 teaspoon vanilla extract

Canola or peanut oil for deep-frying

Chocolate Glaze (page 107)

MAKES ABOUT 10 DONUTS AND THEIR HOLES

In a bowl, sift together the flours, cocoa powder, baking powder, baking soda, and salt. In a large bowl, using an electric mixer set on low speed (use the paddle attachment for a stand mixer), beat the egg and sugar until creamy and pale. Add the buttermilk, melted butter, 1½ teaspoons of the chile powder, and the vanilla and beat until blended. Add the flour mixture and beat, still on low speed, just until the mixture comes together into a soft dough. Cover and refrigerate the dough until firm, at least 30 minutes and up to 1 hour.

Line a baking sheet with paper towels. Pour oil to a depth of 2 inches (5 cm) into a deep-fryer or deep, heavy-bottomed sauté pan and warm over medium-high heat until it reads 360°F (182°C) on a deep-frying thermometer.

On a generously floured work surface, roll out the dough into a circle 10 inches (25 cm) in diameter and ½ inch (12 mm) thick. Using a 3-inch (7.5-cm) round donut cutter, cut out as many donuts as possible. Gather up the donut scraps and repeat rolling and cutting. (For more information on rolling and cutting, see page 13.)

Carefully lower 2–5 donuts or holes into the hot oil and deep-fry until dark brown and crusty on the first side, about 1½ minutes. Turn over and cook until dark brown and crusty on the second side, about 1 minute longer. Transfer to the towel-lined baking sheet. Repeat to fry the remaining donuts and holes, allowing the oil to return to 360°F between batches. (For more information on deep-frying, see page 14.)

Stir the remaining chile powder into the chocolate glaze. When the donuts are cool enough to handle, dip the tops in the glaze, letting any excess glaze drip back into the bowl. Let the glaze set for 10 minutes. Serve right away.

cake
DONUT

double-dipped chocolate donuts

Chocolate yeast-raised donuts frosted with a thick layer of bittersweet chocolate ganache make a sophisticated party treat. Double-dipping the donuts in the chocolate mixture produces the thick topping. For a creative dessert, top each donut with a scoop of coffee- or chocolate-flavored gelato.

¾ cup (6 fl oz/180 ml) whole milk

3 tablespoons unsalted butter

3 cups (15 oz/470 g) all-purpose flour

¼ cup (¾ oz/20 g) unsweetened cocoa powder, preferably Dutch process

⅓ cup (3 oz/90 g) granulated sugar

½ teaspoon salt

1 package (2½ teaspoons) quick-rise yeast

2 large eggs

½ teaspoon vanilla extract

Canola or peanut oil for brushing and deep-frying

Chocolate Ganache (page 103)

MAKES ABOUT
15 DONUTS AND
THEIR HOLES

In a small saucepan over medium heat, combine the milk and butter and heat, stirring, until the butter melts and the mixture is hot but not boiling (about 125°F/52°C on an instant-read thermometer). Remove from the heat. Set aside.

Fit a stand mixer with the paddle attachment. In the mixing bowl, combine 2½ cups (12½ oz/390 g) of the flour, the cocoa powder, sugar, salt, and yeast and beat on low speed to mix. Add the hot milk mixture, raise the speed to medium, and beat until well blended. Add the eggs and vanilla and beat until incorporated, about 2 minutes. Add the remaining ½ cup (2½ oz/7.5 g) flour and beat until well blended and smooth, about 1 minute longer. The dough will not pull away from the sides of the bowl and will still be somewhat sticky, but your finger should come out clean when you insert it into the center. (For a food processor method, see page 10.)

Scrape the dough into a large bowl and cover with a clean kitchen towel. Let the dough stand until well risen and increased in bulk (it may almost double in size), about 45 minutes.

Line a baking sheet with waxed paper and brush the paper with oil. Line a second baking sheet with paper towels.

On a generously floured work surface, roll out the dough into a circle 10 inches (25 cm) in diameter and ½ inch (12 mm) thick. Using a 3-inch (7.5-cm) round donut cutter, cut out as many donuts as possible.

yeast
DONUT

RECIPE CONTINUED ON PAGE 78

double-dipped chocolate donuts
CONTINUED

yeast DONUT

Transfer the donuts and holes to the oiled paper. Gather up the donut scraps and repeat rolling and cutting. (For more information on rolling and cutting, see page 13.) Cover the donuts and holes with a clean kitchen towel and let rise until soft and puffy, about 30 minutes.

Pour oil to a depth of 2 inches (5 cm) into a deep-fryer or deep, heavy sauté pan and warm over medium-high heat until it reads 360°F (182°C) on a deep-frying thermometer. Carefully lower 2–5 donuts or holes into the hot oil and deep-fry until dark brown and crusty on the first side, about 1½ minutes. Turn over and cook until dark brown and crusty on the second side, about 1 minute longer. Transfer to the towel-lined baking sheet. Repeat to fry the remaining donuts and holes, allowing the oil to return to 360°F between batches. (For more information on deep-frying, see page 14.)

If the ganache seems too thick for dipping, transfer it to a stainless-steel bowl and set over (but not touching) a saucepan of simmering water. Heat, stirring until smooth. When the donuts and donut holes are cool enough to handle, dip the tops in the ganache, letting any excess drip back into the bowl. Place on a wire rack and let stand until the ganache sets slightly, about 10 minutes, then dip a second time. Serve right away.

espresso-glazed donuts

Coffee and donuts may be one of the all-time favorite classic combinations, but these dark beauties take the popular duo a step higher by gilding the donuts themselves with a bold espresso glaze. A warm cup of espresso or cappuccino makes the perfect accompaniment.

Canola or peanut oil for brushing and deep frying

Yeast Donut Dough
(page 100)

Espresso Glaze (page 106)

MAKES ABOUT
15 DONUTS AND
THEIR HOLES

Line a baking sheet with waxed paper and brush the paper with oil. Line a second baking sheet with paper towels.

On a generously floured work surface, roll out the dough into a circle 10 inches (25 cm) in diameter and ½ inch (12 mm) thick. Using a 3-inch (7.5-cm) round donut cutter, cut out as many donuts as possible. Transfer the donuts and holes to the oiled paper. Gather up the donut scraps and repeat rolling and cutting. (For more information on rolling and cutting, see page 13.) Cover the donuts and holes with a clean kitchen towel and let rise until soft and puffy, about 30 minutes.

Pour oil to a depth of 2 inches (5 cm) into a deep-fryer or deep, heavy sauté pan and warm over medium-high heat until it reads 360°F (182°C) on a deep-frying thermometer. Carefully lower 2–5 donuts or holes into the hot oil and deep-fry until dark golden, about 1½ minutes. Turn over and cook until dark golden on the second side, about 1 minute longer. Transfer to the towel-lined baking sheet. Repeat to fry the remaining donuts and holes, allowing the oil to return to 360°F between batches. (For more information on deep-frying, see page 14.)

Using a thin metal spatula, spread about 2 tablespoons of the glaze over the top of each donut. Spread the tops of the donut holes with 1–2 teaspoons of the glaze, or dip their tops in it. Let the glaze set for 10 minutes. Arrange the donuts and holes on a platter and serve right away.

yeast
DONUT

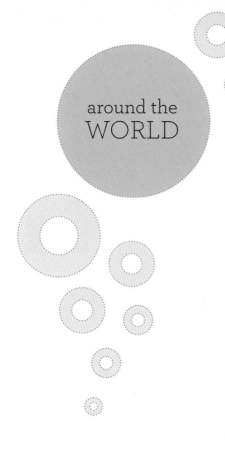

around the
WORLD

lemon-filled beignets

Beignets, a beloved deep-fried but light and airy pastry creation from France, can be made from a yeast dough; a thick batter; or a *pâte à choux*, or cream puff, dough. Lemon curd is called for here, but traditional beignets can also contain any flavor of jam, such as strawberry or blueberry.

⅔ cup (5 fl oz/160 ml) whole milk

2¼ cups (11½ oz/360 g) all-purpose flour

⅓ cup (3 oz/90 g) granulated sugar

¼ teaspoon salt

1 package (2½ teaspoons) quick-rise yeast

6 tablespoons (3 oz/90 g) unsalted butter, at room temperature

1 large egg plus 1 large egg yolk

1 teaspoon grated lemon zest

½ teaspoon vanilla extract

Canola or peanut oil for brushing and deep-frying

Purchased lemon curd

Confectioners' sugar for dusting

MAKES ABOUT 18 BEIGNETS

In a small saucepan over medium heat, warm the milk until hot but not boiling (about 125°F/52°C on an instant-read thermometer). Remove the pan from the heat.

Fit a stand mixer with the paddle attachment. In the mixing bowl, combine the flour, granulated sugar, salt, and yeast and beat on low speed to mix. Add the hot milk, raise the speed to medium, and beat until blended. Add the butter, whole egg and egg yolk, lemon zest, and vanilla and beat until well blended and smooth, about 2 minutes. The dough will not pull away from the sides of the bowl and will still be somewhat sticky, but your finger should come out clean when you insert it into the center. (For a food processor method, see page 10.) Scrape the dough into a large bowl, cover, and let rest for about 10 minutes.

Line a baking sheet with waxed paper and brush the paper with oil. Line a second baking sheet with paper towels.

Lightly grease the palms of your hands with oil. Pull off about 1 teaspoon of the dough and roll it between your palms into a smooth ball, then press into a disk about 2 inches (5 cm) in diameter. Place on the oiled paper. Spoon about 1 teaspoonful of the lemon curd into the center of the dough disk. Make a second dough disk the same way and place on top of the first, stretching the edges over the curd. Pinch the edges to seal tightly. Repeat with the remaining dough and lemon curd. You should have about 18 beignets. Cover with a clean kitchen towel and let rise for 30 minutes.

yeast DONUT

RECIPE CONTINUED ON PAGE 84

lemon-filled beignets

The beignets should look soft and puffy, but will not double in size.

Pour oil to a depth of 2 inches (5 cm) into a deep-fryer or deep, heavy sauté pan and warm over medium-high heat until it reads 365°F (184°C) on a deep-frying thermometer.

Using a spatula, one at a time, transfer 4–5 beignets from the baking sheet to the hot oil, sliding them in gently. Be sure not to overcrowd the pan. The beignets should float to the top and puff to about double their size. Deep-fry until dark golden on the first side, about 1½ minutes. Using tongs, turn and fry until dark golden on the second side, about 1½ minutes longer. Transfer to the towel-lined baking sheet to drain. Repeat to fry the remaining beignets, allowing the oil to return to 365°F between batches. (For more information on deep-frying, see page 14.)

Arrange the beignets on a platter. Using a fine-mesh sieve, dust with confectioners' sugar and serve right away.

yeast
DONUT

creole calas

In the early twentieth century, the morning calls of *"Bella calas, tout chaud!"* ("Beautiful hot *calas*!") could be heard on the streets of New Orleans. These rice fritters were sold by African-American women from baskets balanced on their heads. The calas sellers are now gone, but the popular recipe lives on.

½ cup (2½ oz/75 g) all-purpose flour

¼ cup (2 oz/60 g) firmly packed light brown sugar

1½ teaspoons baking powder

¼ teaspoon salt

⅛ teaspoon freshly grated nutmeg

2 large eggs, lightly beaten

1 teaspoon vanilla extract

2 cups (10 oz/315 g) cooked white rice

Canola or peanut oil for deep-frying

Confectioners' sugar for dusting

Cherry, blueberry, or raspberry jam for serving

MAKES ABOUT 30 CALAS

In a large bowl, whisk together the flour, brown sugar, baking powder, salt, and nutmeg. Using a large spoon, stir in the eggs and vanilla. Stir in the rice just until evenly distributed. Cover and let rest for 10 minutes.

Line a baking sheet with paper towels. Pour oil to a depth of 2 inches (5 cm) into a deep-fryer or deep, heavy sauté pan and warm over medium-high heat until it reads 360°F (182°C) on a deep-frying thermometer.

Using a metal spoon, scoop up a rounded tablespoonful of the batter and drop into the hot oil, or scrape in using a second spoon. Repeat to add 5 or 6 spoonfuls to the oil. Be sure not to overcrowd the pan. The *calas* should float to the top and puff to about double their size. Deep-fry until dark golden on the first side, about 1½ minutes. Using tongs, a wire skimmer, or a slotted spoon, turn and fry until dark golden on the second side, about 1 minute longer. (The thick batter will produce slightly flattened, rather than round, fritters.) Transfer to the towel-lined baking sheet to drain. Repeat to fry the remaining *calas*, allowing the oil to return to 360°F between batches. (For more information on deep-frying, see page 14.)

Arrange the *calas* on a platter. Using a fine-mesh sieve, dust with confectioners' sugar. Serve right away, accompanied by the jam.

cake
DONUT

ricotta zeppole

Various Italian regions boast their own special recipe, but *zeppole* are always famously light in texture. Each year on March 19, *zeppole* are cooked all over Italy to celebrate the feast of Saint Joseph, who answered prayers to end a severe drought during the Middle Ages, and who also reportedly had a way with fritters.

cake
DONUT

Canola or peanut oil
for deep-frying

3 large eggs

⅓ cup (3 oz/90 g)
granulated sugar

½ teaspoon vanilla extract

1 teaspoon grated
orange zest, plus extra
for garnishing

1 cup (8 oz/250 g)
whole-milk ricotta cheese

1¼ cups (6½ oz/200 g)
all-purpose flour

1 teaspoon baking powder

¼ teaspoon salt

Confectioners' sugar
for dusting

MAKES ABOUT
28 ZEPPOLE

Line a large baking sheet with paper towels. Pour oil to a depth of 2 inches (5 cm) into a deep-fryer or deep, heavy sauté pan and warm over medium-high heat until it reads 360°F (182°C) on a deep-frying thermometer.

In a large bowl, whisk together the eggs, granulated sugar, and vanilla until well blended. Add the orange zest and ricotta and whisk to combine. Using a large spoon, stir in the flour, baking powder, and salt and mix just until smoothly incorporated.

Using a metal spoon, scoop up a tablespoonful of the batter and drop gently into the hot oil. Repeat to add 3–5 more spoonfuls to the oil. Be sure not to overcrowd the pan. The *zeppole* should float to the top and puff to about double their size. Deep-fry until dark golden on the first side, about 1 minute. Using tongs, a wire skimmer, or a slotted spoon, turn and fry until dark golden on the second side, about 1 minute longer. Transfer to the towel-lined baking sheet to drain. Repeat to fry the remaining *zeppole*, allowing the oil to return to 360°F between batches. (For more information on deep-frying, see page 14.)

Arrange the *zeppole* on a platter. Using a fine-mesh sieve, dust lightly with confectioners' sugar and orange zest. Serve right away.

cardamom-honey balls

These super-moist, syrup-soaked, bite-sized donuts are one of few types that get even better after standing overnight. In India they are known as *gulab jamun*, distinguished by a dough that has equal parts flour and dry milk powder. Rose water, available in specialty-foods markets, adds a heady floral scent to the syrup.

½ cup (2½ oz/75 g)
all-purpose flour

½ cup (1½ oz/45 g) nonfat
dry milk powder

⅛ teaspoon baking soda

¼ teaspoon salt

2 tablespoons unsalted
butter, melted

¼ cup (2 fl oz/60 ml)
whole milk

Canola or peanut oil for
brushing and deep-frying

MAKES ABOUT
18 DONUT BALLS

cake
DONUT

In a large bowl, whisk together the flour, milk powder, baking soda, and salt. Using a large spoon, stir in the melted butter just until evenly moist and fine crumbs form. Add the whole milk and stir just until the mixture comes together into a soft dough. Cover and let rest for 10 minutes (any remaining streaks of flour and milk powder will be absorbed during resting).

Line a baking sheet with waxed paper and brush the paper with oil. Line a second baking sheet with paper towels. Pour oil to a depth of 2 inches (5 cm) into a deep-fryer or deep, heavy sauté pan and warm over medium-high heat until it reads 350°F (180°C) on a deep-frying thermometer.

Lightly grease the palms of your hands with oil. Pull off about 1 tablespoon of the dough and roll it between your palms into a smooth ball about 1 inch (2.5 cm) in diameter. Place it on the oiled paper. Repeat to shape the remaining dough, spacing the donut balls 1–2 inches (2.5–5 cm) apart on the baking sheet. You should have 18 donut balls.

Using a slotted spoon, one or two at a time, transfer 5–6 donut balls from the baking sheet to the hot oil, sliding them in gently. Be sure not to overcrowd the pan. The donut balls should float to the top and increase in size. Deep-fry until dark golden on all sides, using the slotted spoon to roll them around in the oil as needed to cook them evenly, about 3½ minutes total. Transfer to the paper towel-lined baking sheet to drain. Repeat to fry the remaining donut balls, allowing the oil to return to 350°F between batches. (For more information on deep-frying, see page 14.)

SPICED SYRUP

1 cup (8 oz/250 g) granulated sugar

¼ cup (3 fl oz/90 ml) honey

¼ teaspoon ground cardamom

Pinch of saffron

1 teaspoon rose water

To make the spiced syrup, in a saucepan over medium heat, combine 1 cup (8 fl oz/250 ml) water, the sugar, honey, cardamom, and saffron and bring to a boil, stirring to dissolve the sugar. Cook, stirring often, for 1 minute. Pour into a heatproof bowl and stir in the rose water. Keep warm.

When all the donut balls are fried, transfer them to the pan of warm syrup and stir gently to coat, being careful not to break up the donuts. Let stand in the syrup at room temperature for at least 2 hours. Or, cover, refrigerate, and let the balls stand in the syrup up to overnight.

To serve, spoon 3 donut balls into each of 6 small bowls and spoon any remaining syrup over them. Serve cold or at room temperature.

cake
DONUT

SWEET TIP

Change the flavor of the spiced syrup by adding orange blossom water, sold in specialty-foods stores, in place of the rose water.

churros with chocolate sauce

The long, ridged horns of the Churro breed of Spanish sheep inspired the elongated shape of the well-loved Latin American donuts called churros. Made by piping strips of *pâte à choux* (a classic pastry borrowed from France) into hot oil, they are often served with cups of warm chocolate sauce for dipping.

CHOCOLATE SAUCE

1 cup (8 fl oz/250 ml) half-and half

3 tablespoons unsalted butter, cut into cubes

⅓ cup (1 oz/30 g) unsweetened cocoa, preferably Dutch process

½ cup (4 oz/125 g) granulated sugar

1 teaspoon vanilla extract

CHURROS

½ cup (4 oz/125 g) unsalted butter

½ teaspoon salt

1 cup (5 oz/150 g) all-purpose flour

3 large eggs, at room temperature

½ teaspoon vanilla extract

Canola oil for deep-frying

⅔ cup (5 oz/150 g) granulated sugar

1 teaspoon ground cinnamon

MAKES ABOUT
35 CHURROS

To make the chocolate sauce, in a saucepan over medium-low heat, combine the half-and-half, butter, cocoa powder, and sugar and bring to a simmer, whisking to dissolve the sugar and cocoa powder. Cook for 1 minute, whisking constantly. Remove from the heat and stir in the vanilla. Pour the sauce into a heatproof bowl. Set aside and cover to keep warm.

To make the churros, cut the butter into ½-inch (12-mm) cubes. In a saucepan over medium heat, combine 1 cup (8 fl oz/250 ml) water, the butter, and salt and bring to a boil, stirring to melt the butter. Add the flour all at once and stir vigorously with a wooden spoon until the flour is incorporated and the dough pulls away from the sides of the pan in a ball. Reduce the heat to low and cook, stirring constantly, for 1 minute. The dough will continue to pull away from the pan sides in a large clump.

Scrape the dough into a large bowl. Using an electric mixer set on medium speed (use the paddle attachment for a stand mixer), beat until the dough forms large clumps, about 1 minute. Add the eggs one at a time, beating until smooth after each addition. Beat in the vanilla.

Line a baking sheet with paper towels. Pour oil to a depth of 2 inches (5 cm) into a deep-fryer or deep, heavy sauté pan and warm over medium-high heat until it reads 360°F (182°C) on a deep-frying thermometer.

Fit a pastry bag with a ½-inch (12-mm) star tip and spoon the dough into the bag. Dip a large, wide spatula into the hot oil, letting any excess drip back

pâte à
CHOUX

RECIPE CONTINUED ON PAGE 92

pâte à
CHOUX

into the fryer. Pipe 2 dough strips, each 6–7 inches (15–18 cm) long, onto the spatula, spacing them about 1 inch (2.5 cm) apart. Slide the spatula into the hot oil and let the dough slide off into the oil. Repeat to add 2–4 more strips to the oil. Be sure not to overcrowd the pan. The churros should float to the top and increase in size. Deep-fry until dark golden on the first side, about 2 minutes. Using tongs, a wire skimmer, or a slotted spoon, turn and fry until dark golden on the second side, about 1½ minutes longer. Transfer to the towel-lined baking sheet to drain. Repeat to fry the remaining churros, allowing the oil to return to 360°F between batches. (For more information on deep-frying, see page 14.)

In a large, shallow bowl, mix together the sugar and cinnamon. When the churros are cool enough to handle, roll them in the cinnamon-sugar to coat generously. (You may have extra cinnamon-sugar, but this makes for easier coating.) Arrange the churros on a platter and serve right away with the warm chocolate sauce for dipping.

bombolini

Bombolini are bite-sized, jam-filled donuts made from a traditional *pâte à choux* (cream-puff dough). They resemble small, light jelly donuts that, as the name suggests, explode in your mouth like a tiny, sweet bomb. Be sure to use a smooth jam or one with fruit pieces small enough to fit through the piping tip.

1 cup (8 fl oz/250 ml) whole milk

½ cup (4 oz/125 g) unsalted butter, cut into ½-inch (12-mm) cubes

½ teaspoon salt

1 cup (5 oz/150 g) all-purpose flour

3 large eggs, at room temperature

½ teaspoon vanilla extract

Canola or peanut oil for deep-frying

½ cup (4 oz/125 g) granulated sugar

¾ cup (7½ oz/235 g) best-quality apricot, plum, or cherry jam

MAKES ABOUT 30 BOMBOLINI

In a saucepan over medium heat, combine the milk, butter, and salt and bring to a boil, stirring to melt the butter. Add the flour all at once and stir vigorously with a wooden spoon until the flour is incorporated and the dough pulls away from the sides of the pan in a ball. Reduce the heat to low and cook, stirring constantly, for 1 minute.

Scrape the dough into a large bowl. Using an electric mixer set on medium speed (use the paddle attachment for a stand mixer), beat until the dough forms large clumps, about 1 minute. Add the eggs one at a time, beating until smooth after each addition. Beat in the vanilla. Cover and refrigerate the dough until firm, about 1 hour.

Line a baking sheet with paper towels. Pour oil to a depth of 2 inches (5 cm) into a deep-fryer or deep, heavy sauté pan and warm over medium-high heat until it reads 360°F (182°C) on a deep-frying thermometer. Using a 1-tablespoon ice cream scoop, scoop up a round of dough and drop into the hot oil. Repeat to add 3–5 more rounds to the oil. Deep-fry until golden on the first side, about 2 minutes. Turn and fry until golden on the second side, about 1½ minutes longer. Transfer to the towel-lined sheet. Repeat to fry the remaining bombolini, allowing the oil to return to 360°F between batches.

Put the sugar on a large plate. When the bombolini are cool enough to handle, roll them in the sugar to coat on all sides. Fit a pastry bag with a ¼-inch (6-mm) round tip, and spoon the jam into the bag. Using the tip of a small, sharp knife, cut a ¼-inch (6-mm) slit in the side of each bombolini. Press the tip of the pastry bag gently into the slits and pipe about 1 teaspoon of the jam into each bombolini. Serve right away.

pâte à CHOUX

chocolate-glazed french crullers

French crullers, identified by their famous fluted rings, have a light and airy texture produced by their age-old *pâte à choux*, which uses only flour, butter, water, and eggs. Chocolate glaze is used here, but cinnamon, maple, or vanilla glaze (see pages 105 and 106) also make delectable options.

4 tablespoons (2 oz/60 g) unsalted butter, cut into small pieces

½ teaspoon granulated sugar

½ teaspoon salt

½ cup (2½ oz/75 g) all-purpose flour

2 large eggs, at room temperature

½ teaspoon vanilla extract

Canola or peanut oil for brushing and deep-frying

⅔ cup (5 fl oz/160 ml) Chocolate Glaze (page 107)

MAKES 8 CRULLERS

In a saucepan over medium heat, combine ½ cup (4 fl oz/125 ml) water, the butter, sugar, and salt and bring to a boil, stirring to melt the butter. Add the flour all at once and stir vigorously with a wooden spoon until the flour is incorporated and the dough pulls away from the sides of the pan in a ball. Reduce the heat to low and cook, stirring constantly, for 1 minute. The dough will continue to pull away from the pan sides in a large clump.

Scrape the dough into a large bowl. Using an electric mixer set on medium speed (use the paddle attachment for a stand mixer), beat until the dough forms large clumps, about 1 minute. Add the eggs one at a time, beating until smoothly blended after each addition. Add the vanilla and beat until smooth.

Pour oil to a depth of 2 inches (5 cm) into a deep-fryer or deep, heavy sauté pan and warm over medium-high heat until it reads 360°F (182°C) on a deep-frying thermometer.

Line a baking sheet with paper towels. Line a second baking sheet with waxed paper. Cut eight 4-inch (10-cm) squares of waxed paper and arrange them on the paper-lined baking sheet. Brush the paper squares with oil. Fit a pastry bag with a ½-inch (12-mm) star tip and fill the bag with the dough. Pipe a 3-inch circle of dough onto each of the 8 squares of paper.

When the oil is hot, carefully turn over one of the dough-topped paper pieces and slide the dough circle into the hot oil. Repeat to add 1 or 2 more dough circles to the oil. Be sure not to overcrowd the pan. The crullers

pâte à CHOUX

RECIPE CONTINUED ON PAGE 96

chocolate-glazed french crullers
CONTINUED

should increase in size. Deep-fry until dark golden on the first side, about 2 minutes. Using tongs, a wire skimmer, or a slotted spoon, turn and fry until dark golden on the second side, about 1½ minutes longer. Transfer to the towel-lined baking sheet, fluted side up, to drain. Repeat to fry the remaining crullers, allowing the oil to return to 360°F between batches. (For more information on deep-frying, see page 14.)

Using a spoon or a small squeeze bottle filled with the glaze, drizzle the glaze in a back-and-forth pattern over the top of each cruller. Let the glaze set for 10 minutes. Arrange on a platter and serve right away.

pâte à
CHOUX

banana fritters

Banana fritters are a Southeast Asian treat consisting of bananas dipped in batter and then deep-fried into a tiny, tasty treat. If you can't find palm sugar, also known as coconut sugar, brown sugar can be substituted. For an indulgent dessert, serve them alongside coconut-flavored ice cream or mango sorbet.

½ cup (2½ oz/75 g) all-purpose plain flour

½ cup (2 oz/60 g) rice flour

½ teaspoon baking powder

Salt

3 tablespoons granulated sugar

1 cup (8 fl oz/250 ml) coconut milk

3 tablespoons unsalted peanuts, toasted (page 100) and finely chopped

2 tablespoons unsweetened shredded dried coconut, toasted (page 100)

2½ teaspoons palm sugar

1 tablespoon unsalted butter

4 large, ripe bananas, peeled and halved crosswise

1 teaspoon fresh lime juice

Canola or peanut oil for deep-frying

Confectioners' sugar for dusting

MAKES ABOUT
8 FRITTERS

In a large bowl, sift together the all-purpose and rice flours, baking powder, and a pinch of salt. Stir in the granulated sugar. Whisk in the coconut milk until the batter just comes together. Cover and refrigerate for 30 minutes.

To make the filling, in a food processor, combine the peanuts, toasted coconut, palm sugar, and a pinch of salt and pulse until finely minced. Add the butter and pulse several times until the mixture has the consistency of cooked oatmeal.

Place the bananas in a large bowl and toss with lime juice. Using a small, sharp knife, cut a lengthwise slit 3 inches (7.5 cm) long in each banana piece, forming a pocket. Using a spoon, add about 1 teaspoon of the filling into each pocket.

Line a baking sheet with paper towels. Pour oil to a depth of 2 inches (5 cm) into a deep-fryer or deep, heavy sauté pan and heat to 375°F (190°C) on a deep-frying thermometer. Using tongs, dip 4–5 banana pieces into the batter, shaking off the excess. Carefully slide the bananas into the hot oil and fry until dark golden on the first side, about 2 minutes. Turn and fry until dark golden on the second side, about 1½ minutes longer. Transfer to the towel-lined baking sheet. Repeat to fry the remaining bananas, allowing the oil to return to 375°F between batches. (For more information on deep-frying, see page 14.)

Arrange the fritters on a platter. Using a fine-mesh sieve, dust generously with confectioners' sugar. Serve right away.

cake
DONUT

sopaipillas

Sopaipillas, made from a dough similar to a piecrust, were originally a South American specialty but are now popular in New Mexico and Texas. When the flaky dough is deep-fried, it puffs up dramatically. The donuts, with their many air pockets, make perfect vehicles for the honey that is drizzled inside.

2 cups (10 oz/315 g) all-purpose flour

1 teaspoon granulated sugar

1 teaspoon baking powder

½ teaspoon salt

1 tablespoon cold unsalted butter, cut into small pieces

1 tablespoon cold vegetable shortening, cut into small pieces

Canola or peanut oil for deep-frying

Confectioners' sugar for dusting

¾ cup (9 oz/280 g) honey

MAKES ABOUT 30 SOPAIPILLAS

cake DONUT

In a large bowl, using an electric mixer set on low speed (use the paddle attachment for a stand mixer), combine the flour, granulated sugar, baking powder, and salt and beat on low speed to mix. Stop the mixer, add the butter and shortening pieces, and beat, on low speed, just until the butter and shortening pieces are no larger than small peas and the mixture looks mealy, about 20 seconds. With the machine running, slowly pour in ½ cup (4 fl oz/125 ml) water and beat just until the dough is evenly moist and begins to come together into a mass, about 20 seconds longer. Add more water, 1 tablespoon at a time, if needed. The dough will form large clumps and pull away from the sides of the bowl, but will not form a ball. Cover the dough and let rest for 20 minutes.

Line a large baking sheet with paper towels. Pour oil to a depth of 2 inches (5 cm) into a deep-fryer or deep, heavy sauté pan and warm over medium-high heat until it reads 365°F (184°C) on a deep-frying thermometer.

Turn the dough out onto a generously floured work surface. Using a floured rolling pin, roll out the dough into a 9-by-10-inch (23-by-25-cm) rectangle. Using a sharp knife, cut the dough into 2-inch (5-cm) squares or triangles. You should have about 30 sopaipillas.

Using a wide spatula, one at a time, carefully transfer 3 or 4 sopaipillas from the work surface to the hot oil, sliding them in gently. Be sure not to overcrowd the pan. The sopaipillas should float to the top and puff in the center or slightly off center. Deep-fry until dark golden on the first side, about 3 minutes. Using a slotted spoon, turn and fry until dark golden on the second side, about 1½ minutes longer. Using tongs, transfer the sopaipillas to the towel-lined baking sheet to drain. Repeat to fry the remaining sopaipillas, allowing the oil to return to 365°F between batches. (For more information on deep-frying, see page 14.)

Arrange the sopaipillas on a platter. Using a fine-mesh sieve, dust with confectioners' sugar. Serve right away, passing the honey at the table. Instruct diners to either tear off a small piece of sopaipilla and drizzle honey into the puffed opening, or drizzle honey over the top before eating.

cake
DONUT

basic recipes and techniques

yeast donut dough

¾ cup (6 fl oz/180 ml) whole milk

3 tablespoons unsalted butter

3¼ cups (16½ oz/515 g) all-purpose flour

⅓ cup (3 oz/90 g) granulated sugar

½ teaspoon salt

1 package (2½ teaspoons) quick-rise yeast

2 large eggs

½ teaspoon vanilla extract

MAKES ONE 10-INCH (25-CM) DOUGH ROUND

In a small saucepan over medium heat, combine the milk and butter and heat, stirring, until the butter is melted and the mixture is hot but not boiling (about 125°F/52°C on an instant-read thermometer). Remove from the heat.

Fit a stand mixer with the paddle attachment. In the mixing bowl, combine 2½ cups (12½ oz/390 g) of the flour, the sugar, salt, and yeast and beat on low speed to mix. Add the hot milk mixture, raise the speed to medium, and beat until well blended. Add the eggs and vanilla and beat until fully incorporated, about 2 minutes. Add the remaining ¾ cup (4 oz/125 g) flour and beat until the dough is well blended and smooth, about 1 minute longer. The dough will not pull away from the sides of the bowl and will still be somewhat sticky. (If you don't have a stand mixer, turn to page 10 for a food processor method.)

Scrape the dough into a large bowl and cover with a clean kitchen towel. Let stand in a warm place until well risen and increased in bulk (it may almost double in size), about 45 minutes. Use the dough right away, as directed in the recipe.

toasting coconut

Preheat the oven to 325°F (165°C). Spread shredded dried coconut in a single layer in a large rimmed baking sheet. Bake, stirring occasionally for even browning, until the coconut is fragrant and the color deepens, about 5–10 minutes. Transfer to a plate to cool.

toasting nuts

ON THE STOVETOP Spread the nuts in an even layer in a small sauté pan. Toast the nuts over medium heat, stirring them often, until fragrant and lightly browned, about 10–15 minutes. Transfer to a plate to cool.

IN THE OVEN Preheat the oven to 325°F (165°C). Spread the nuts in an even layer in a large rimmed baking sheet. Bake, stirring occasionally for even browning, until the nuts are fragrant and lightly browned, about 10–15 minutes. Transfer to a plate to cool.

fillings, glazes, and toppings

meyer lemon custard

1 cup (8 fl oz/250 ml) whole milk

3 large egg yolks

½ cup (4 oz/125 g) granulated sugar

4 teaspoons cornstarch

2 tablespoons unsalted butter, at room temperature

½ teaspoon grated Meyer lemon zest

¼ cup (2 fl oz/60 ml) fresh Meyer lemon juice

1 teaspoon vanilla extract

MAKES ABOUT 1½ CUPS (12 FL OZ/375 ML)

In a saucepan over medium heat, warm the milk until small bubbles appear around the edges of the pan. Remove from the heat. In a heatproof bowl, combine the egg yolks, sugar, and cornstarch and whisk until smooth. Slowly whisk in the hot milk until thoroughly blended. Return the egg-yolk mixture to the saucepan and place over medium heat. Cook, whisking constantly, until the mixture comes to a boil and thickens, about 3 minutes. Continue cooking, stirring constantly, for 1 minute longer to cook. Pour the custard through a sieve into a bowl. Stir in the butter, lemon zest and juice, and vanilla. Press a piece of plastic wrap onto the surface of the custard to prevent a skin from forming and poke a few holes in the plastic with the tip of a knife to allow steam to escape. Refrigerate until chilled, at least 2 hours or up to overnight.

banana custard

1 cup (8 fl oz/250 ml) whole milk

3 large egg yolks

⅓ cup (3 oz/90 g) granulated sugar

4 teaspoons cornstarch

2 tablespoons unsalted butter, at room temperature

2 ripe bananas, mashed

1 teaspoon vanilla extract

MAKES ABOUT 1½ CUPS (12 FL OZ/375 ML)

In a saucepan over medium heat, warm the milk until small bubbles appear along the edges of the pan. Remove from the heat. In a heatproof bowl combine the egg yolks, sugar, and cornstarch and whisk until smooth. Slowly whisk in the hot milk until blended. Return the egg-yolk mixture to the saucepan and place over medium heat. Cook, whisking constantly, until the mixture comes to a boil and thickens, about 3 minutes. Continue cooking, stirring constantly, for 1 minute longer to cook completely. Pour the custard through a fine-mesh sieve into a clean bowl. Stir in the butter, bananas, and vanilla. Press a piece of plastic wrap directly onto the surface of the custard to prevent a skin from forming and poke a few holes in the plastic with the tip of a knife to allow steam to escape. Refrigerate until well chilled, for at least 2 hours or up to overnight.

vanilla custard

1 cup (8 fl oz/250 ml) whole milk

3 large egg yolks

⅓ cup (3 oz/90 g) granulated sugar

4 teaspoons cornstarch

2 tablespoons unsalted butter,
at room temperature

1 teaspoon vanilla extract

MAKES ABOUT 1½ CUPS (12 FL OZ/375 ML)

In a saucepan over medium heat, warm the milk until small bubbles appear around the edges of the pan. Remove from the heat. In a heatproof bowl, combine the egg yolks, sugar, and cornstarch and whisk until smooth. Slowly whisk in the hot milk until thoroughly blended. Return the egg-yolk mixture to the saucepan and place over medium heat. Cook, whisking constantly, until the mixture comes to a boil and thickens, about 3 minutes. Continue cooking, stirring constantly, for 1 minute longer to cook completely. Pour the custard through a fine-mesh sieve into a clean bowl. Stir in the butter and vanilla. Press a piece of plastic wrap directly onto the surface of the custard to prevent a skin from forming and poke a few holes in the plastic with the tip of a sharp knife to allow steam to escape. Refrigerate until well chilled, at least 2 hours or up to overnight.

chocolate ganache

1 cup (8 fl oz/250 ml) heavy cream

1 tablespoon unsalted butter

9 oz (280 g) bittersweet chocolate,
finely chopped

1 teaspoon vanilla extract

MAKES ABOUT 2½ CUPS (20 FL OZ/625 ML)

In a saucepan over low heat, combine the cream and butter and heat, stirring, until the butter is melted, tiny bubbles form, and the mixture is hot but not boiling (175°F/80°C on an instant-read thermometer). Remove from the heat, add the chocolate, and let stand for about 30 seconds to allow the chocolate to soften. Whisk until the chocolate is melted and the ganache is smooth. Stir in the vanilla. Pour the ganache into a metal bowl and use right away.

chocolate cream filling

2 oz (60 g) bittersweet chocolate, chopped

¾ cup (6 fl oz/180 ml) cold heavy cream

2 tablespoons confectioners' sugar

1 tablespoon unsweetened cocoa powder,
preferably Dutch process

½ teaspoon vanilla extract

MAKES ABOUT 1½ CUPS (12 FL OZ/375 ML)

Place the chocolate in the top pan of a double boiler or a heatproof bowl and place over, but not touching, a pan of boiling water. Stir until melted and smooth. Remove from the heat and set aside.

In a bowl, combine the cream, confectioners' sugar, cocoa powder, and vanilla. Using an electric mixer set on medium-high speed, beat until stiff peaks form. In another bowl, combine half of the sweetened whipped cream with the melted chocolate and whisk to combine. Using a rubber spatula, gently fold in the remaining whipped cream just until no white streaks remain. Use right away.

meyer lemon glaze

6 tablespoons (3 oz/90 g) unsalted butter, melted

2½ cups (10 oz/315 g) confectioners' sugar

2 tablespoons fresh Meyer lemon juice

3 tablespoons hot water, plus more as needed

½ teaspoon grated Meyer lemon zest

MAKES ABOUT 3 CUPS (24 FL OZ/750 ML)

In a bowl whisk together the melted butter, confectioners' sugar, lemon juice, and 3 tablespoons hot water until smooth. Whisk in 1–2 teaspoons more hot water if needed to give the glaze a thin consistency. Stir in the lemon zest. Use right away.

orange-flower glaze

6 tablespoons (3 oz/90 g) unsalted butter, melted

2½ cups (10 oz/315 g) confectioners' sugar

1 teaspoon vanilla extract

¾ teaspoon orange-flower water

5 tablespoons (3 fl oz/80 ml) hot water, plus more as needed

MAKES ABOUT 3 CUPS (24 FL OZ/750 ML)

In a bowl, whisk together the melted butter, confectioners' sugar, vanilla, orange-flower water, and 5 tablespoons hot water until smooth. Whisk in 1–2 teaspoons more hot water if needed to give the glaze a thin, light consistency. Use right away.

cinnamon-orange glaze

2 cups (8 oz/250 g) confectioners' sugar

1 teaspoon ground cinnamon

1 teaspoon light corn syrup

1 teaspoon grated orange zest

3 tablespoons hot water, plus more as needed

MAKES ABOUT 2½ CUPS (20 FL OZ/625 ML)

In a bowl, stir the confectioners' sugar, cinnamon, corn syrup, orange zest, and 3 tablespoons hot water until well blended. Stir in 1–2 teaspoons more hot water if needed to give the glaze a thin, light consistency. Use right away.

cinnamon-apple glaze

1 cup (4 oz/125 g) confectioners' sugar

½ teaspoon ground cinnamon

2 tablespoons apple cider or apple juice, plus more as needed

MAKES ABOUT 1¼ CUPS (10 FL OZ/310 ML)

In a bowl, stir together the confectioners' sugar, cinnamon, and 2 tablespoons apple cider until well blended. Stir in 1–2 teaspoons more cider if needed to make a smooth glaze that is easy to spread but thick enough to cling to the donuts. Use right away.

cinnamon glaze

6 tablespoons (3 oz/90 g) unsalted butter, melted

2½ cups (10 oz/315 g) confectioners' sugar

1 teaspoon ground cinnamon

1 teaspoon vanilla extract

5 tablespoons (3 fl oz/80 ml) hot water,
plus more as needed

MAKES ABOUT 3 CUPS (24 FL OZ/750 ML)

In a bowl, whisk together the melted butter,
confectioners' sugar, cinnamon, vanilla, and
5 tablespoons hot water until smooth. Whisk in
1–2 teaspoons more hot water if needed to give
the glaze a thin, light consistency. Use right away.

coconut glaze

6 tablespoons (3 oz/90 g) unsalted butter, melted

2½ cups (10 oz/315 g) confectioners' sugar

1 teaspoon vanilla extract

½ teaspoon coconut extract

5 tablespoons (3 fl oz/80 ml) hot water,
plus more as needed

MAKES ABOUT 3 CUPS (24 FL OZ/750 ML)

In a bowl, whisk together the melted butter,
confectioners' sugar, vanilla and coconut extracts,
and 5 tablespoons hot water until smooth. Whisk
in 1–2 teaspoons more hot water if needed to give
the glaze a thin, light consistency. Use right away.

vanilla glaze

6 tablespoons (3 oz/90 g) unsalted butter, melted

2½ cups (10 oz/315 g) confectioners' sugar

1 teaspoon vanilla extract

5 tablespoons (3 fl oz/80 ml) hot water,
plus more as needed

MAKES ABOUT 3 CUPS (24 FL OZ/750 ML)

In a bowl, whisk together the melted butter,
confectioners' sugar, vanilla, and 5 tablespoons hot
water until smooth. Whisk in 1–2 teaspoons more
hot water if needed to give the glaze a thin, light
consistency. Use right away.

thick vanilla glaze

2 cups (8 oz/250 g) confectioners' sugar

1 teaspoon light corn syrup

1 teaspoon vanilla extract

3 tablespoons hot water, plus more as needed

MAKES ABOUT 2 CUPS (16 FL OZ/500 ML)

In a bowl, stir together the confectioners' sugar,
corn syrup, vanilla, and 3 tablespoons hot water.
Stir in 1–2 teaspoons more hot water if needed
to make a smooth glaze that is easy to spread but
thick enough to cling to the donuts. Use right away.

maple glaze

1 cup (4 oz/125 g) confectioners' sugar

¼ cup (3 oz/85 g) pure maple syrup

3 tablespoons heavy cream

MAKES ABOUT 2 CUPS (16 FL OZ/500 ML)

In a bowl, stir together the confectioners' sugar and maple syrup until well blended. Add the cream and whisk until smooth. Add a few more drops of cream or water if needed to make a smooth glaze that is easy to spread but thick enough to cling to the bars. Use right away.

caramel glaze

¾ cup (6 fl oz/180 ml) heavy cream

1 cup (7 oz/220 g) plus 2 tablespoons firmly packed light brown sugar

3 tablespoons light corn syrup

½ teaspoon salt

1 teaspoon vanilla extract

MAKES ABOUT 2 CUPS (16 FL OZ/500 ML)

In a heavy saucepan over medium heat, combine the cream, brown sugar, and corn syrup and heat, stirring often, until the brown sugar is dissolved and the mixture is smooth. Raise the heat to medium-high, bring to a boil, and cook, stirring constantly, for 2 minutes. Remove from the heat and stir in the salt and vanilla. Set aside and let stand at room temperature; the glaze will thicken as it cools. (The glaze will keep, covered in the refrigerator, for up to 2 days). If the glaze is cold, reheat gently over low heat just until soft enough to spread.

espresso glaze

2 cups (8 oz/250 g) confectioners' sugar

2 teaspoons instant espresso powder dissolved in 2 teaspoons water

1 teaspoon light corn syrup

¼ teaspoon vanilla extract

3 tablespoons hot water, plus more as needed

MAKES ABOUT 2½ CUPS (20 FL OZ/625 ML)

In a bowl, stir together the confectioners' sugar, espresso, corn syrup, vanilla, and 3 tablespoons hot water until well blended. Stir in 1–2 teaspoons more hot water if needed to make a smooth glaze that is easy to spread but thick enough to cling to the donuts. Use right away.

sticky toffee glaze

1 cup (8 fl oz/250 ml) heavy cream

¾ cup (6 oz/185 g) firmly packed dark brown sugar

1 teaspoon molasses

MAKES ABOUT 1¼ CUPS (10 FL OZ/310 ML)

In a saucepan over medium heat, combine the cream, brown sugar, and molasses and bring to a gentle boil, stirring to dissolve the brown sugar. Cook, uncovered, stirring often, until the mixture is reduced to about 1¼ cups (10 fl oz/310 ml), about 30 minutes. Adjust the heat as needed to maintain a gentle boil (just several large bubbles breaking the surface). Remove from the heat and set the sauce aside at room temperature to cool, about 1 hour. Use right away.

chocolate glaze

⅓ cup (3 fl oz/80 ml) heavy cream

4 tablespoons (2 oz/60 g) unsalted butter,
cut into ½-inch (12-mm) cubes

3 tablespoons light corn syrup

4 oz (125 g) semisweet chocolate, finely chopped

1 teaspoon vanilla extract

MAKES ABOUT 1 CUP (8 FL OZ/250 ML)

In a saucepan over medium heat, combine the
heavy cream, butter, and corn syrup and cook,
stirring, until the butter melts and the mixture
is hot but not boiling. Remove the pan from
the heat and add the chocolate. Let stand for
about 30 seconds, then stir until the chocolate
is completely melted and the glaze is smooth.
Stir in the vanilla. Let the glaze cool until
thickened, about 20 minutes. Use right away.

almond crunch

1 large egg white

1¼ cups (5 oz/150 g) sliced almonds

2 tablespoons granulated sugar

MAKES ABOUT 1½ CUPS (12 OZ/375 G)

Preheat the oven to 325°F (165°C). Line a rimmed
baking sheet with parchment paper. In a bowl,
whisk the egg white until foamy, about 30 seconds.
Add the almonds and stir to coat them evenly with
the egg white. Sprinkle the sugar evenly over the
nuts and stir to mix well. Spread the nuts into a
single layer on the prepared baking sheet. Bake,
stirring once, until the nuts look golden and dry,

about 15 minutes. Remove from the oven and stir
the nuts to loosen them from the paper. Let cool
on the baking sheet; the nuts will become crisp as
they cool. Use right away.

sugar-and-spice topping

½ cup (4 oz/125 g) sugar

1½ teaspoons freshly ground pepper

1 teaspoon grated lemon zest

1 teaspoon kosher or sea salt

MAKES ABOUT ¾ CUP (6 OZ/185 G)

In a wide, shallow bowl, combine the sugar, pepper,
lemon zest, and salt and stir to mix until combined.
Use right away.

streusel topping

¾ cup (4 oz/125 g) all-purpose flour

⅓ cup (3 oz/90 g) granulated sugar

⅓ cup (2½ oz/75 g) firmly packed
light brown sugar

½ teaspoon ground cinnamon

¼ teaspoon salt

4 tablespoons (2 oz/60 g) unsalted butter, melted

MAKES ABOUT 1½ CUPS (12 OZ/375 G)

In a large bowl, stir together the flour, granulated
sugar, brown sugar, cinnamon, and salt. Add the
melted butter and stir just until crumbs form and
the mixture is evenly moistened. Use right away.

index

a

Almonds
    Almond Crunch, 107
    Chocolate–Almond Crunch
       Donuts, 73–74
    toasting, 100
Apples
    Apple Fritters, 37
    Cider Glaze, 27
    Cider-Glazed Donuts, 26–27
    Cinnamon-Apple Glaze, 104

b

Bacon-Maple Donuts, 65–66
Baked Cherry-Streusel Donuts, 53
Bananas
    Banana Cream Donuts, 71
    Banana Custard, 102
    Banana Fritters, 97
Beignets, Lemon-Filled, 81–82
Blueberry–Sour Cream Drops, 28
Bombolini, 91
Brown Sugar Donuts, 68–70
Buttermilk Donuts,
    Old-Fashioned, 22

c

Cake donuts, 9
    Apple Fritters, 37
    Baked Cherry-Streusel Donuts, 53
    Banana Fritters, 97
    Cardamom-Honey Balls, 88–89
    Chocolate-Chile Donuts, 75
    Chocolate-Hazelnut Fritters, 67
    Cider-Glazed Donuts, 26–27
    Cinnamon-Sugar Donut
       Holes, 32–33
    Creole Calas, 85

Devil's Food Donuts, 41
Honey-Cornmeal Donuts, 54
Lemon–Olive Oil Donuts, 47
Maple-Bacon Donuts, 65–66
Old-Fashioned Buttermilk
    Donuts, 22
Pistachio-Orange Donuts, 49–50
Potato Donuts, 38
Ricotta Zeppole, 86
Sopaipillas, 98–99
Sour Cream–Blueberry Drops, 28
Sticky Toffee Donuts, 63
Toasted Coconut Donuts, 31
Triple Ginger Donuts, 59
Calas, Creole, 85
Caramel
    Caramel Glaze, 106
    Salted Caramel–Pecan
       Donuts, 61–62
Cardamom-Honey Balls, 88–89
Cherry-Streusel Donuts,
    Baked, 53
Chile-Chocolate Donuts, 75
Chocolate
    Chocolate–Almond Crunch
       Donuts, 73–74
    Chocolate-Chile Donuts, 75
    Chocolate Cream Filling, 103–4
    Chocolate Ganache, 103
    Chocolate Glaze, 107
    Chocolate-Glazed French
       Crullers, 93–94
    Chocolate-Hazelnut Fritters, 67
    Chocolate Sauce, 90
    Churros with Chocolate
       Sauce, 91–92
    Devil's Food Donuts, 41
    Double-Dipped Chocolate
       Donuts, 77–78

Churros with Chocolate Sauce, 91–92
Cider
    Cider Glaze, 27
    Cider-Glazed Donuts, 26–27
    Cinnamon-Apple Glaze, 104
Cinnamon
    Cinnamon-Apple Glaze, 104
    Cinnamon Glaze, 105
    Cinnamon-Orange Glaze, 104
    Cinnamon-Sugar Donut
       Holes, 32–33
    Cinnamon Twists, 35–36
Coconut
    Banana Fritters, 97
    Coconut Glaze, 105
    Toasted Coconut Donuts, 31
    toasting, 100
Cornmeal-Honey Donuts, 54
Creole Calas, 85
Crullers, Chocolate-Glaze
    French, 93–94
Custards
    Banana Custard, 102
    Meyer Lemon Custard, 102
    Vanilla Custard, 103

d

Dates
    Sticky Toffee Donuts, 63
Deep-frying, 10, 14
Devil's Food Donuts, 41
Donut cutters, 10, 13
Donuts. See also individual
    recipes and categories
    deep-frying, 14
    history of, 6
    rolling and cutting, 13
    tools for making, 10

weldon**owen**

415 Jackson Street, Suite 200, San Francisco, CA 94111

www.wopublishing.com

DONUTS

Conceived and produced by Weldon Owen Inc.

Copyright © 2010 Weldon Owen Inc.

All rights reserved, including the right of reproduction
in whole or in part in any form.

Color separations by Embassy Graphics
Printed and bound in China by 1010 Printing, Ltd.

First printed in 2010

10 9 8 7 6

·Library of Congress Cataloging-in-Publication
data is available.

ISBN-13: 978-1-74089-982-6
ISBN-10: 1-74089-982-2

Weldon Owen is a division of

BONNIER

WELDON OWEN INC.

CEO and President Terry Newell
VP, Sales and Marketing Amy Kaneko
Director of Finance Mark Perrigo

VP and Publisher Hannah Rahill
Executive Editor Jennifer Newens
Editor Donita Boles
Assistant Editor Becky Duffett

Creative Director Emma Boys
Senior Designer Ashley Lima
Designer Lauren Charles
Junior Designer Anna Grace

Production Director Chris Hemesath
Production Manager Michelle Duggan
Color Manager Teri Bell

Photographer Lauren Burke
Food Stylist Robyn Valarik
Prop Stylist Sara Slavin

ACKNOWLEDGMENTS

Weldon Owen wishes to thank the following people for their generous support in producing this book:
Carrie Bradley, Linda Bouchard, Sean Franzen, and Victoria Woollard.